AF570725

Joy
and
Remembrance

Joy and Remembrance

Commentary on the Sabbath Eve Liturgy

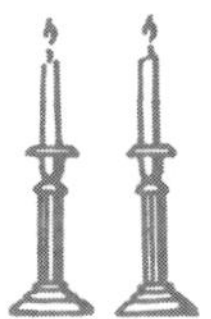

Max Arzt

HARTMORE HOUSE
New York & Bridgeport

HARTMORE HOUSE, Inc.
1363 Fairfield Avenue
Bridgeport, Conn. 06605

Manufactured in the United States of America

LIBRARY OF CONGRESS CATALOGING IN PUBLICATION DATA

Arzt, Max.
Joy and remembrance.

Includes bibliographical references.
1. Jews. Liturgy and ritual. Sabbath prayers—Commentaries. I. Title.
BM675.S3Z726 296.4′1 79-63435
ISBN 0-87677-147-9

For my

Children,

Grandchildren,

and Great Grandchildren

PUBLISHER'S NOTE

Dr. Max Arzt was immersed in the preparation of Joy and Remembrance, *reviewing his notes and manuscript material, when he passed away.*

Undoubtedly, Dr. Arzt would have wanted to deal with some of the book's themes in greater detail. Fortunately, however, we have before us a beautiful collection of comments, explanatory notes, excerpts from classical sources, and personal interpretations.

Conveying the meaning and spirit of the Sabbath Eve liturgy, the book reflects as well the wisdom and grace of a beloved teacher and spiritual leader.

Preface

The Sabbath is the cornerstone of Jewish life—in concept and practice. Described by tradition as a *remembrance* of Creation and as a *remembrance* of the Exodus, it has been observed over the centuries as a day of *Joy*.

Uplifting the otherwise dreary life of the Jew in difficult times, conferring meaning and majesty in good times and bad, the Sabbath is the quintessential Jewish institution; for here the ideal of *Simḥah Shel Mitzvah,* the joyous performance of sacred duties, is linked to a rich tapestry of interwoven ceremonies, procedures, liturgies, and creaturely delights.

For many Jews in our day, trying to relate to the traditional liturgy of the Sabbath (and, indeed, of other occasions) poses problems. The metaphors and imagery of the Prayer Book are often difficult to grasp; at times, the concepts seem alien to our modes of thought. In addition, many of those who wish to understand the liturgy are not in a position to relate it to an experiential base of involvement with the Sabbath as a living reality.

Yet, we feel compelled to grapple with the ancient words of the liturgy. For, insights of great profundity, embedded in the liturgy, can be made to speak beyond the boundaries of their time and the limitations of their pristine form.

Moreover, quite apart from the liturgy's importance in the worship life of the individual and the community, it is an indispensable source for an understanding of the fundamental character of traditional Judaism, whose value-concepts and convictions are most clearly reflected in the *Siddur*.

This book aims to present a *sampling* of explanatory, historical, and theological material either directly related to the liturgy or prompted by reflections on it. It attempts to present the material in a manner comprehensible to the thoughtful lay person. The format and variety of *types* of material used reflect the author's hope that *Joy and Remembrance* will also be used for *group* study and discussion—with additional examples of the various genres of interpretive material presented by the discussion leader and/or by members of the group who prepare for particular sessions.

Joy and Remembrance is intended as a companion volume to the author's larger *Justice and Mercy* (a commentary on the liturgy of the High Holy Days) in which certain concepts and passages common to all Jewish liturgy are discussed. In the present work, too, some of the material presented relates to topics and questions likely to carry the inquiry beyond the Sabbath.

Having benefited from the wisdom of colleagues and friends, it is my hope that *Joy and Remembrance* will be a useful resource for others who are involved in *learning* and *living* the *Shabbat*.

Contents

KABBALAT SHABBAT: Welcoming the Sabbath

MAARIV: Sabbath Evening Service

THE KABBALAT SHABBAT PSALMS AND HYMNS

Rabbi Simeon ben Yoḥai taught: The Sabbath said to the Holy One, blessed be He, "O Master of the universe, every living being You created has its mate and each day has its companion, but I am alone." Whereupon the Holy One, blessed be He, said to her, "The Congregation of Israel will be your mate." When the Israelites stood at Mount Sinai, the Holy One, blessed be He, said to them, "Remember what I said to the Sabbath: 'The Congregation of Israel will be your mate.' Therefore the fourth commandment begins with the word, 'Remember' " (Exodus 20:8).

Pesikta Rabbati 117b; Genesis Rabbah 11:8

It was the practice of Rabbi Ḥanina to put on his best clothes before the Sabbath would set in, and say, "Come, let us welcome Queen Sabbath."

Talmud, Shabbat 119a

Rabbi Yannai would put on his best garments and say, ''Come, O bride. Come, O bride.''

Talmud, Shabbat 119a

Rabbi Hamnuna said: He who offers the Sabbath Eve prayers and recites the verses beginning with, ''And the heaven and the earth were finished'' (Genesis 2:1-3), is considered in the Torah as though he had become a partner in Creation, for one can vocalize the word *Vayekhullu* [''heaven and earth were finished''], as *Vayekhallu*, ''*they* [man and God], finished the Creation.''

Talmud, Shabbat 119b

KABBALAT SHABBAT

INTRODUCTION

In the middle of the sixteenth century, the mystics of Safed, enraptured with the Rabbinic characterization of the Sabbath as Israel's bride, introduced the practice of welcoming the arrival of the Sabbath with the recitation of six psalms—symbolic of the six weekdays. The recital of the psalms was followed by the singing of a hymn, *Lekhah Dodi* ("Come, my beloved, to meet the Bride; let us welcome the Sabbath day"). The author of this beautiful hymn was Solomon Halevi Alkabez, a brother-in-law of the Kabbalist Moses Cordovero, who was a pupil of Joseph Karo. Karo was the author of the *Shulḥan Arukh,* which became the most widely accepted Code of Jewish Law. Cordovero held the position of *Dayyan* (judge) in the Safed community, and the way of life he recommended for his Kabbalistic associates is outlined in a list of moral precepts contained in a manuscript drawn up by him, which was published in 1908 by Solomon Schechter.

The following abstracts of these precepts are offered in Schechter's essay on Safed:

> *Cordovero enjoins the Associates not to divert their thoughts from the words of the Torah and things holy, so that their hearts become the abode of the* Shekhinah; *not to be betrayed into anger, as anger delivers man into the power of sin; not to speak evil of any creature, including animals; never to curse any being, but to accustom oneself to bless even in moments of anger; never to take an oath, even on the truth; never to speak an untruth under any condition; to be careful not to be included among the four classes excluded from the Divine Presence, namely the hypocrites, the liars, the scoffers, and the talebearers; not to indulge in banquets except on religious occasions. They are enjoined to mingle their minds with the minds of their fellow-men (that is, not to stand aloof from the world, but to share both in its joys and in its sorrows), and to behave in a kindly spirit toward their fellow-men, even though they be transgressors; to meet with one of the Associates for one or two hours every day for the purpose of discussing matters spiritual; to talk over with an Associate every Friday the deeds accomplished during the week, and then set out for the reception of Queen Sabbath; to pronounce Grace in a loud voice, letter by letter and word by word, so that the children at the table can repeat after the reader; to confess their sins before every meal and before going to sleep; to use the sacred language when speaking with the Associates, and to let this be always the language of conversation on Sabbath with other scholars as well. In another set of precepts drawn up by Alkabez, dating from this time and probably also meant for the guidance of these Associates, we have the ordinance that the students should rebuke or admonish each other, but the person admonished or rebuked must not make any reply in his defense before the lapse of three days.**

---

* S. Schechter, *Studies in Judaism,* second series (Philadelphia, 1908), pp. 238-39.

To the Safed Kabbalists, the Sabbath was a living reality, an eagerly awaited guest welcomed every Friday, after an absence of six days, with the ineffable joy and the expectant love with which a groom meets his bride. The *Lekhah Dodi* hymn proclaims an invincible faith in the dawn of the Messianic era, when Israel, the harried and harassed lover of Queen Sabbath, would be restored to its sacred homeland and when the Divine Presence would return to its abode in Zion. The poem consists of a mosaic of Biblical phrases overlaid with Talmudic allusions. Almost every phrase can be traced to a Biblical or Talmudic source. Yet, in the words of Israel Abrahams, "the hymn stands out as a strikingly original composition, fresh, fragrant and full of new charm. This literary phenomenon can have few exact parallels."

Alkabez's wording of *Lekhah Dodi* was inspired by an earlier version composed by Moses ben Machir, another sixteenth-century Kabbalist.

That version, which appeared in the first edition of Moses ben Machir's Seder ha-Yom *(Venice, 1599), carries the same* Lekhah Dodi *refrain, and one stanza,* "Bo-i ve-Shalom ateret baalah" *("Come in peace, crown of her Master"), appears word for word in Alkabez's poem. In his youth, Moses ben Machir lived in Safed, and he writes as follows in his* Seder ha-Yom:

> *When going out to greet the Sabbath, it is preferable to be accompanied by a fellow student or pupil; two or three together being proper. . . . In former times the sages would say to each other or to their pupils, "Come, let us go out to greet the Bride," and then they would go to some open field away from their home, or to a garden or to a courtyard, there the Sabbath would be received; but it is not necessary to go to the outskirts of the town. At the place where they welcome the Sabbath Bride they recite six psalms (Psalms 95, 96, 97, 98, 99, and Psalm 29) and then they recite a poem of seven stanzas. . . .* (A. Berliner, *Ketavim Nivḥarim* [Jerusalem, 1945], p. 43.)

Moses ben Machir's Lekhah Dodi *contains seven stanzas, though Alkabez's version of it contains eight since it is structured as an acrostic of his Hebrew name* Shelomo ha-Levi.

Despite the reluctance of many liturgical authorities to approve of Kabbalistic compositions and practices, the *Kabbalat Shabbat* psalms and the *Lekhah Dodi* hymn have won widespread recognition. They are found in most liturgical rites, though the Sephardic rite contains only Psalm 29 and the *Lekhah Dodi* hymn. The original outdoor feature of the *Kabbalat Shabbat* accounts for the practice of rising and facing westward when the concluding stanza is recited, as if the worshipers were about to greet the arrival of a welcome guest. Because the *Kabbalat Shabbat* liturgy is a late addition to the prescribed evening service, it has been the practice in some congregations for the reader to lead this part of the service from the center *Bimah* and then to move to the reader's stand for the *Barekhu* which marks the actual commencement of the evening service.*

We can surmise what prompted the Kabbalists to include the six psalms of the *Kabbalat Shabbat* in the Friday evening service. Each of them alludes to God as King, Creator, and Provider of the world, and together they were seen to envision and foreshadow a perfect era of universal accord, when the God of Israel would be acclaimed by all men and all nations as the universal King. In that blissful era, which they awaited with a compelling faith, Creation, which has been polluted and defiled by man's dereliction and moral corrosion, will at last be perfected by the Kingship of God.

Man has thus far failed in his divinely ordained duty of serving as God's "partner" in the perfection of Creation. The concept that man has a role to play in Creation is implied in the Rabbinic comment on the importance of reciting *Vayekhullu* on Sabbath Eve. The Rabbis suggest that *Vayekhullu* when vocalized *Vayekhallu* would mean that they, man and God, are engaged in the completion of the Creation. "Everything that God created," say the Rabbis in another passage, "is in need of perfection . . . even man is in need of perfection" (Genesis Rabbah 11:6). The word used here for perfection is *Tikkun,* and to the Kabbalists *Tikkun* was a key to their intricate system of mystical speculations.

The Kabbalists taught that every man is in a state of exile

---

* On the inclusion of Psalms 92 and 93 in the *Kabbalat Shabbat* service, see pp. 28 and 61-62.

because he has shrunk in spiritual stature to become immersed in a morass of moral corruption and pollution. The people of Israel is in *Galut* (exile), and it can achieve its *Tikkun* (redemption) by returning to God from whom it became alienated when it ignored His commandments. To speed the end of the *Galut,* the Jew needs to find his *Tikkun* through a life of prayer, piety, and good deeds. By fulfilling the commandments of the Torah, the individual Jew can wend his way back to the original splendor which was his when he had *D'vekut,* continuous adhesion to God. He needs to lift his life out of the *Klippot* (shells) that cause confusion and disorder and that disturb the harmony of Creation. By his *Tikkun,* the individual Jew not only reclaims his alienated self but also liberates the *Shekhinah* (Divine Presence) from its state of exile, thus accelerating the arrival of the Messianic era of Israel's restoration to the Holy Land. But it is not the Jew alone who needs redemption. Every human being needs a *Tikkun*. The *Tikkun* of the "nations of the world" requires the individual's conformance to the Noachian laws which, according to Talmudic teaching, consist of seven basic laws deemed to be obligatory on all "Sons of Noah."

The seven laws are:

(1) Not to worship idols;
(2) Not to blaspheme the name of God;
(3) To establish courts of justice;
(4) Not to murder;
(5) Not to steal;
(6) Not to commit adultery or incest;
(7) Not to eat flesh torn from a living animal.

Talmud, Sanhedrin 56b

Thus, every human being needs to undergo a process of rectification, purification, and restoration to the primordial state of purity which was Adam's before he defied the command of God.*

To the Kabbalists these psalms were seen as depicting and

* Gershom Scholem, *Major Trends in Jewish Mysticism* (Schocken, 1941), pp. 283-286.

predicting the millennial Sabbath that the Rabbis envisioned when they said, that "this world is only like the eve of the Sabbath whereas the world to come would be like the Sabbath itself" (Ruth Rabbah 3:3). Indeed, a Mishnaic statement speaks of a "day which will be wholly one of Sabbath and rest in eternity" (Mishnah, Tamid 7:4).

* * *

A different but no less intriguing exposition of these psalms is offered by Yehezkel Kaufmann in his monumental and seminal work on the Bible.* He disputes and refutes the interpretations read into these psalms by the German Bible critics, H. Gunkel and S. Mowinckel. Gunkel claimed they reflected prophetic visions similar to those expressed in Isaiah (Chapters 40 through 66) regarding the redemption of Israel in the remote future or even "at the end of time." These visions, Gunkel contended, represented the highest stage in the maturing of the religion of Israel out of a tribal, parochial concept of God to that of the God of all mankind. The world-wide jubilation they express is eschatological and otherworldly in tone. Mowinckel, on the other hand, contended that these psalms were annual cultic dramatizations rooted in pagan atavisms celebrating the enthronement of God after His victory over mythological primeval monsters that had to be subdued before God could turn chaos into cosmos.

Kaufmann demolishes these interpretations by marshalling formidable textual and contextual evidence that the psalms reflect a period in the religion of Israel preceding the Babylonian exile. Their exultant universalism is an expression of an overpowering conviction that God is the Author of Creation and that He rules over the destinies of men and nations. True, the nations do not know and therefore do not recognize the Kingship of God and His concern for the welfare of all nations, but the psalmist feels God's universal sway so strongly that he summons the nations to join

---

* Kaufmann, *Toldot ha-Emunah ha-Yisraelit* (Jerusalem, 1953), pp. 716-727; see also Kaufmann, *The Religion of Israel,* ed. Moshe Greenberg (Chicago, 1960), p. 118.

Israel in acknowledging and celebrating the Kingship and majesty of God. In his ecstasy, he proclaims, "Let the sea roar, and the fullness thereof; the world and they that dwell therein. Let the floods clap their hands; let the mountains sing for joy together" (Psalms 98:7-8; cf. 96:11-12).

Kaufmann argues that the psalms do not speak of God coming to "judge the earth" in a hoped for millennial era. They rather depict God the Creator as reigning *now* over all nature and over all nations.

For the Lord is a great God
And a great King above all gods,
In whose hands are the depths of the earth;
The heights of the mountains are His also. (95:3-4)

Say among the nations: The Lord reigneth;
The world also is established that it cannot be
moved. (96:10)

The Lord reigneth: let the earth rejoice;
Let the multitude of isles be glad. (97:1)

The Lord hath made known His salvation [deliverance],
His righteousness has He revealed in the sight of the
nations. (98:2)

The Lord is great in Zion:
And He is high above all the peoples.
Let them praise Thy name as great and awful [awesome];
Holy is He. (99:2-3)

The Lord sat enthroned at the flood;
The Lord sitteth as King forever. (29:10)

Two types of occasions inspired such enthusiasms. The first type was the celebration of some triumphant event in the experience of the people of Israel. In words absolute and final, Israel urges the nations to join it in praising God for His kindness to His people, since a victory for God's people constitutes convincing proof of His omnipotence. Such a resounding call to join in tumultuous rejoicing is struck in Psalm 117:

O praise the Lord all ye nations,
Laud Him all ye peoples,
For His mercy is great toward us,
And the truth [faithfulness] of the Lord endureth forever.
Hallelujah. (117:1-2)

Among verses in the six Sabbath Eve psalms carrying this motif are the following:

The Lord reigneth; let the earth rejoice;
Let the multitude of isles be glad.
Clouds and darkness are round about Him;
Righteousness and justice are the foundation of His throne.
A fire goeth before Him,
And burneth up His adversaries round about. . . .
The heavens declared His righteousness
And all the peoples saw His glory. (97:1-3, 6)

O sing unto the Lord a new song;
For He hath done marvelous things;
His right hand, and His holy arm,
Hath wrought salvation [victory] for Him.
The Lord hath made known His salvation [victory];
His righteousness hath He revealed in the sight of the nations.
He hath remembered His mercy and His faithfulness toward the house of Israel;
All the ends of the earth have seen the salvation [victory] of our God. (98:1-3)

The Lord reigneth; let the peoples tremble;
He is enthroned upon the cherubim;
Let the earth quake.
The Lord is great in Zion;
And He is high above all peoples.
Let them praise Thy name as great and awful [awesome];
Holy is He. (99:1-3)

The second type of situation that may have induced proclamations of the universal sway of God's Kingship was the celebration of New Year. All of mute nature, all men, and all nations are the recipients of the bounties of God. When the psalmist declares, "For God is come to judge the earth," he does not refer to celestial assizes at which chastisement would be decreed upon the peoples. Kaufmann shows that the root *Shafat,* which is usually translated "to judge" in these psalms, has other shades of meaning such as: "to govern, to provide for, and to sustain." This is the evident force of *Tishpot* in Psalm 67, which should be rendered as follows:

> God is gracious unto us, and He has blessed us;
> He has caused His face to shine toward us; Selah.
> That Thy way may be known on the earth,
> Thy deliverance among all nations.
> Let the peoples praise Thee, O God.
> Let the peoples praise Thee, all of them.
> Let the nations be glad and sing for joy;
> For Thou dost provide [Hebrew: *Tishpot*] the peoples with kindness,
> And the nations on earth, Thou dost sustain; Selah.
> Let the peoples praise Thee, O God;
> Let the peoples praise Thee, all of them.
> The earth has yielded her produce,
> Our God, our own God has blessed us.
> Our God has blessed us,
> And let all the ends of the earth worship Him. (67:2-8)

The recognition of God as Creator and Provider, is the main theme of Psalms 96 and 98. Here are some illustrations which take into consideration Kaufmann's observation on the special nuance on *Lishpot* and *Yishpot* in 96:13 and 98:9, and also on *Yadin* in 96:10:*

> Say among the nations: The Lord reigneth.
> The world also is established that it cannot be moved;
> He sustains [Hebrew: *Yadin* = *Yishpot*]** the peoples with kindness.

* For an illuminating discussion of Kaufmann's observations, see H. L. Ginsberg, "A Strand in the Cord of Hebraic Hymnody," *Eretz-Israel, Albright Volume* (Jerusalem, 1969), pp. 46-47.

** See H. L. Ginsberg, *op. cit.,* p. 46b.

Let the heavens be glad, and let the earth rejoice;
Let the sea roar and the fullness thereof;
Let the field exult, and all that is therein;
Then shall all the trees of the forest sing for joy
Before the Lord, for He has come;
He has come to provide for [*Lishpot*] the earth;
He provides for [*Yishpot*] the earth with kindness
And for the peoples with His graciousness. (96:10-13)

Let the sea roar, and the fullness thereof;
The world, and they that dwell therein;
Let the floods clap their hands;
Let the mountains sing for joy together
Before the Lord, for He has come to provide for [*Lishpot*] the earth;
He provides for [*Yishpot*] the world with kindness
And for the peoples with favor. (98:7-9)

There are six *Kabbalat Shabbat* psalms, one for each of the six days of the week.

In an insightful lecture on the Sabbath Eve liturgy, Leon J. Liebreich shows that originally only Psalms 92 and 93 were recited in the Sabbath Eve service before *Barekhu*. According to the Midrash, Adam was the author of both psalms: he composed Psalm 93 (the psalm for Friday) on the day he was created, which was before his sin, and Psalm 92 after he repented. Accordingly, the Talmudic explanation for the recital of Psalm 93 on Fridays by the Levites is that it opens with the words: "The Lord reigneth" because it proclaims that God was clothed in majesty and splendor on Friday when creation was completed (Talmud, Rosh Hashanah 31a). For this reason it was deemed suitable for recitation also on the Sabbath after Psalm 92, which does not directly refer to the Kingship of God, since the Sabbath is an appropriate time for Israel to express the hope that God's Kingship be made manifest once more. Liebreich goes on to show that at the end of the sixteenth century, when the Kabbalists selected additional Psalms to emphasize the idea of God's Kingship, Psalm 94 was *not* chosen (because it contains no reference to the Kingship concept), while

Psalms 95, 96, 97, 98, and 99 were chosen since each has such a reference:

"For the Lord is a great God,
And a great King above all gods." (95:3)

"Say among the nations: 'The Lord reigneth.' " (96:10)

"The Lord reigneth; let the earth rejoice." (97:1)

"With trumpets and sound of the horn
Shout ye before the King, the Lord." (98:6)

"The Lord reigneth; let the peoples tremble." (99:1)

For the sixth psalm, necessary to correspond to the sixth day of the week that precedes the Sabbath, Psalm 29 was chosen because it too speaks of God as King:

"The Lord sat enthroned at the flood;
Yea, the Lord sitteth as King forever." (29:10)

In fact, in the Sephardic rite only Psalm 29 is recited before *Lekhah Dodi,* while in the Ashkenazic rite all the six psalms are included.

The inclusion of Psalm 29 in all the liturgical rites was warranted by the special significance attributed to it in the Talmud. Talmudic tradition has it that the Torah was given on a Sabbath (Talmud, Shabbat 86b). In the Pentateuch's account of the giving of the Torah at Mount Sinai (Exodus 19:1-20:18) the word *Kol* (voice) is mentioned seven times, and the word also occurs seven times in Psalm 29. The psalm was thus associated with the revelation at Sinai (Yalkut, Tehillim 709). In the closing verse, which reads, "The Lord will give strength to His people," the word for strength *(Oz)* was interpreted to refer to the Torah.* The association of this psalm with the giving of the Torah accounts for the custom of standing during its recitation, and for chanting this psalm on Sabbath morning as the recessional for returning the Torah to the ark, a custom which arose in the twelfth century.

---

* The passage from Talmud, Zevaḥim 116a, cited on p. 52, is illustrative of how this psalm was seen as a dramatization of the Sinaitic revelation.

The psalm depicts a manifestation of nature in words of matchless beauty and power. A thunderstorm originating in the Mediterranean Sea travels eastward on the mainland with a terrifying and devastating effect. In this awesome spectacle, the poet sees powerful evidence of the sovereignty of God over the forces of nature. He calls on the celestial beings, the angelic retinue of the Creator, to render to God the glory due to Him. Amidst the shattering peals of the thunder and the lightning, he hears the voice of the Lord (29:1-4), which shatters the cedars of the Lebanon forest and makes them skip like calves. With increasing fury the storm strikes further east and the tall trees of the Sirion forest skip like a wild-ox (29:5-6). Flames of fire appear, and they are a manifestation of that same divine voice. The hurricane finally reaches the Syrian wilderness of Kadesh. In its trail it has made the hinds calve and stripped the forests bare. But in His Temple all exclaim ''Glory,'' for throughout these convulsions of nature God remains enthroned as King and He lends majesty *(Oz)* to His people and confers upon them the blessing of peace. (29:11)*

All the six *Kabbalat Shabbat* psalms are characterized by a passionate awareness of God as the Creator, of His special relationship to the people of Israel, of His Kingship over all nations and over the forces of nature. Through the centuries they stimulated in the faithful Jew a mood of hope and a sense of victorious living in the face of an unknown and unpredictable future and a present which might otherwise sink him in an abyss of despair. In their welcome to Queen Sabbath, the people ushered in a day of blessed respite from their desperate struggle for existence. They borrowed hope from the future and that hope recharged their courage. In their dedication of the Sabbath day to the celebration and proclamation of God's Kingship, they enshrined the hope that all men and peoples would in the future join in acclaiming God's rule:

---

* An analysis of the high antiquity of Psalm 29 and of the meaning it assumed when it was adapted by the psalmist, is to be found in H. L. Ginsberg's article, *op. cit.*, pp. 45-46.

Before God created the world, there was none but God and His great name. Before man was created, heaven and earth, angels and planets, waters and herbs and trees, birds and beasts all joined in a chorus of praise to God. But even the angels could only partly testify to the glory of God for they had an absolute disability to commit sin. Only mortal man endowed with freedom of will could make real the ideal, "One generation shall laud Thy works to another" (Psalms 145:4).

Hence when the Holy One, blessed be He, consulted the Torah as to the creation of the world, she answered, "Master of the universe, if there be no host, over whom will the King reign and if there be no peoples praising Him, where is the glory of the King?"

Pirke de Rabbi Eliezer, ch. 3

KABBALAT SHABBAT

Lekhu nerannenah ladonai לְכוּ נְרַנְּנָה לַה'

"O come, let us sing unto the Lord" (Psalm 95)

COMMENTS ON THE TEXT

"Let us come before His presence with thanksgiving,
Let us shout for joy unto Him with psalms." (95:2)

To come before the presence of God meant to visit the Temple at Jerusalem where God had His earthly abode. Though the whole earth is full of His glory (Isaiah 6:3), man experiences the Divine Presence most intimately when he visits the Temple. The Temple, like the Tabernacle in the wilderness, aimed to provide man with a heightened sense of the nearness of God: "Let them make Me a sanctuary that I may dwell among them" (Exodus 25:8). In Rabbinic discourse, the indwelling presence of God was called *Shekhinah,* from the Hebrew word meaning "to dwell."

"Let us shout for joy . . ." (95:2)

Pilgrims from all parts of the land and from the Diaspora as well, would visit the Temple. The experience was not solely of awesome solemnity, but one brimming with joy and jubilation. People, accompanied by their friends, brought thanksgiving offerings to the Temple. A homesick pilgrim, who, because of his distance from Jerusalem could not visit the Temple, expressed his yearning recollections in these words:

> These things I remember and pour out my soul within me,
> How I passed on with the throng and led them to the house of God,
> With the voice of joy and praise,
> A multitude keeping holyday. (Psalms 42:5)

"O come, let us bow down and bend the knee,
Let us kneel before the Lord our God." (95:6)

Kneeling and prostration were gestures of submission and obedience to royalty. When the prophet Nathan presented himself before David, "He bowed down before the king with his face to the ground" (I Kings 1:23). In prayer, kneeling and prostration were symbolic of man's homage to God. Thus, in the account of the impressive exercises at the dedication of the first Temple we are told, "When Solomon had made an end of praying all this prayer and supplication unto the Lord, he rose from before the altar of the Lord, from kneeling on his knees with his hands spread forth toward heaven" (I Kings 8:54). In the same terms a prophet envisions the future when God's rule will be universally acknowledged: "Unto Me every knee shall bow, every tongue shall swear" (Isaiah 45:23). Here our psalmist invites all the pilgrims to enter the Temple court and "to kneel before the Lord our God." In the *Alenu* prayer with which every service concludes, we say, "Whereas we kneel and bow down and prostrate* ourselves before the supreme King of kings, the Holy One."

Kneeling and prostration in Jewish worship

The Bible makes frequent reference to bowing, kneeling, and prostration as postures of homage in worship.** The Mishnah

---

* That *Modim* here means "we prostrate ourselves" is convincingly demonstrated by Saul Lieberman in *Tosefta Ki-feshutah, Moed,* p. 696.

** Genesis 24:26, 24:28; Leviticus 9:24; I Kings 8:54; Isaiah 1:15; Psalms 22:30; Daniel 6:11.

records that everyone who entered the second Temple prostrated himself opposite the thirteen gates of the Temple, with hands and knees extended (Mishnah, Shekalim 6:1). Another passage tells that the thirteen prostrations were made as gestures of deliverance from the Syrian Greeks who had made thirteen breaches in the latticed railing inside the Temple Mount (Mishnah, Middot 2:3). While these thirteen prostrations were deemed to be optional for the congregation, the priests (Kohanim) were required to make the full prostration after every sacrifice (Mishnah, Tamid 6:1-2; Tosefta, Shekalim 2:17). On Yom Kippur, all who heard the High Priest pronounce the Ineffable Name "threw themselves on the ground and prostrated themselves" (Mishnah, Yoma 6:2). One of the ten wonders of the Temple was that the people standing pressed together, yet had room to prostrate themselves at ease (Mishnah, Avot 5:5).

After the destruction of the Temple, prostration was not carried over to the synagogue worship. It was restricted only to the *Alenu* introduction to the *Malkhuyot* prayers on Rosh Hashanah and to the *Avodah* service of Yom Kippur, both of which were regarded as reminiscent of Temple days. The restriction on kneeling and prostration was justified by the technical claim that kneeling and prostration on the stone floors of Palestinian synagogues would be in violation of "You shall not . . . place figured stones in your land to worship on" (Leviticus 26:1). In Babylonia, where the synagogues did not have stone pavements, the people would prostrate themselves on the ground. Thus, when Rav returned to Babylonia after an absence in Palestine, he remained standing when the others in the synagogue threw themselves on the ground, though they did not extend hands and feet as was the ancient practice in the Temple. But the strictures on the Palestinian Jews against kneeling and prostration are explained differently by Louis Ginzberg as having been due to the desire to differentiate worship in the Synagogue from that in the Church, which had meticulously adopted all the postures and gestures then in vogue at the Temple. In Babylonia the Jews were not so strict about kneeling because there were few Christians there.

The Palestinian authorities limited even bowing in prayer to the beginning and conclusion of the first blessing of the *Amidah* and to the beginning and conclusion of *Modim* (Tosefta, Berakhot 1:8). Excessive bending of the body was deemed objectionable, and one who did so when leading the congregation in prayer was taught not to repeat the practice (*ibid.*). Rabbi Akiva took more liberties when he recited privately the supplementary prayers that followed the *Amidah*. He would begin praying in one corner of the synagogue but end up in a corner on the other side due to the many genuflections and prostrations he had made (Tosefta, Berakhot 3:7). In Geonic times the *Nefillat Appayyim** (literally, "falling on the face"), which was originally a full prostration, was restricted to forward bowing of the head while reclining on the arm.

That the restriction on kneeling and prostration at prayer was induced by Christianity's adoption of these gestures can be seen from the attempt made by Rabbi Abraham, the son of Maimonides, to introduce a number of prostrations during the *Kaddish,* during *Barekhu,* during the *Kedushah* of the *Yotzer* (which follows *Barekhu* in the morning service), and after the *Shema*. Such postures were also current in Islam's worship, but the need to deviate from them was not as keenly felt. The postures were practiced through the centuries by pious Jews in Moslem lands.**

"For He is our God,
And we are the people of His pasture
And the flock of His hand." (95:7)

In the first part of the psalm, God is celebrated as the Creator and Sovereign of all that is on the earth and in the depths of the sea. But we worship Him and bow to Him not only because He is the Creator but also because we feel intimately related to Him as the people He shepherds. The same juxtaposition of His role as Creator and Protector is expressed in Psalm 100: "Shout unto the Lord, all the earth. Serve the Lord with gladness; come before His presence with singing. Know that the Lord alone is God; it is He that hath made us, and we are His, His people, and the flock of His pasture" (100:1-3).

---

* During the *Taḥanun* after the weekday *Amidah*.

** Naphtali Wieder, *Islamic Influences on the Jewish Worship* (Hebrew), East and West Library (1947), pp. 47-64.

"Today, if you would but hearken to His voice." (95:7)

The observance of rituals will be accepted only if prayer and sacrifice are accompanied by moral integrity. Isaiah tells the people that God cannot endure "iniquity with the solemn assembly" (Isaiah 1:13). The prophets emphasized that rite must be accompanied by right, that true religion demands ethical rectitude. This thought is especially underscored in Psalms 15 and 24.

Psalm 15 begins with the question:

> Lord, who shall sojourn in Thy tabernacle,
> Who shall dwell upon Thy holy mountain? (15:1)

The Targum paraphrases the question as follows: "Lord, who *is fit* [*Hami*] to sojourn in Thy tabernacle, who *is fit* to dwell upon Thy holy mountain?"

The person who meets the requirements for admission to the Temple is described in this psalm as one who walks with integrity, who practices righteousness, and who speaks the truth in his heart. He is a person who has no malice on his tongue, never wrongs another person and never heaps disgrace on a neighbor. He scorns contemptible persons and respects people of noble character (*Hebrew:* who fear the Lord). He swears to his own hurt and does not retract, he does not put his money out to usury, and he never accepts a bribe against the innocent (15:2-5).

Psalm 24 opens with a similar question, as if it were being asked by a priest who is welcoming pilgrims at the gates of the Temple. First he reminds them that God has no need of any material gifts for,

> The earth is the Lord's and the fullness thereof;
> The world and they that dwell therein.
> For it was He that founded it upon the seas,
> And established it upon the floods. (24:1-2)

Then the priest asks:

> Who shall [may] ascend the mountain of the Lord?
> And who shall [may] stand in His holy place? (24:3)

He then proceeds to state that the worshiper who is acceptable to

God is one "Who has clean hands and a pure heart, who has never taken God's name in vain and has never sworn deceitfully." (24:4)

"Harden not your heart as at Meribah,
As in the day of Massah in the wilderness." (95:8)

The reference here is to events mentioned in Exodus 17:1-7 and Numbers 20:1-13. The mention of such past events helps the people reflect on the lessons to be drawn from their collective experience. A popular knowledge of the contents of the Torah can be assumed from such casual references to past events.

"That they shall not enter My rest."* (95:11)

"My rest" means the Temple, the earthly abode of God where worshipers felt His nearness though they knew that His living presence transcended the symbolic representations of His accessibility.

SELECTED RABBINIC COMMENTS

"Let us come before His presence with thanksgiving." (95:2)

Thanksgiving is the noblest expression of religious feeling; it is ranked higher than sacrificial offerings, for Scripture says, "But I, with loud thanksgiving will sacrifice to You" (Jonah 2:10).

Midrash Tehillim 95:1

"For He is our God,
And we are the people of His pasture,
And the flock of His hand." (95:7)

When are we His people? When we are "the sheep of His pasture." When we are [peaceful] like the sheep of His pasture,

---

* The Hebrew for "rest" is *Menuḥah,* and this same word applies to Zion and the Temple site, as, for example, in this passage:

"For the Lord has chosen Zion; He has desired it for His habitation:
This is My resting place forever; here will I dwell for I have desired it."
(Psalms 132:13-14)

then we are His people, as Scripture says, "And ye My sheep, the sheep of My pasture, are men, and I am the Lord your God" (Ezekiel 34:31).

But when we are wild like lions, God rejects us, for Scripture says, "My heritage [My own people] is become unto Me as a lion in the forest . . . therefore I have hated [rejected] her" (Jeremiah 12:8).

Midrash Tehillim 95:2

"Today, if you would but hearken to His voice." (95:7)

Rabbi Joshua ben Levi met Elijah at the mouth of the cave of Rabbi Simeon ben Yoḥai. He asked Elijah, "When will Messiah come?" Elijah replied, "Go and ask him." "But where is he?" "At the gate of Rome," he said. "How shall I identify him?" "He sits among the poor who suffer from body sores. All the others remove the bandages from their wounds and then they all bind them up again but Messiah unbinds them and bandages them one by one, lest he be suddenly summoned and be delayed in returning." Then Rabbi Joshua asked him, "When is the Master [Messiah] coming?" He replied, "*Today*." Rabbi Joshua then went back to Elijah and Elijah asked him, "What did the Messiah say to you?" . . . "He spoke an untruth to me!" said Rabbi Joshua. "He said he would come *today* but he has not come." Whereupon Elijah responded: "He meant, '*Today!* if you would but hearken to His voice.' "

Talmud, Sanhedrin 98a

"Today [This day], if you would but hearken to His voice." (95:7)

Rabbi Levi said: Were the people of Israel to observe just one Sabbath day as it should be kept, they would be immediately redeemed, for Scripture says, "This 'day,' if you would but hearken to His voice" (95:7), and it also says, "Remember the Sabbath 'day' and keep it holy" (Exodus 20:8).

Midrash Tehillim 95:2;
cf. Talmud, Shabbat 118b

Shiru ladonai shir ḥadash שִׁירוּ לַה׳ שִׁיר חָדָשׁ
"O sing unto the Lord a new song" (Psalm 96)

COMMENTS ON THE TEXT

"O sing unto the Lord a new song,
Sing unto the Lord, all the earth." (96:1)

A "new song" marked the celebration of a momentous national victory or the rapturous greeting of an abundant harvest at the beginning of a new year. Since all nations are the beneficiaries of God's bounty and goodness, the poet ecstatically calls on all the earth (*i.e.,* on all humanity) to join the chorus of praise and thanksgiving:

Ascribe unto the Lord, ye kindreds of the peoples,
Ascribe unto the Lord glory and strength.
Ascribe unto the Lord the glory due to His name. (96:7-8)

SELECTED RABBINIC COMMENTS

"O sing unto the Lord a new song,
Sing unto the Lord, all the earth.
Sing unto the Lord, bless His name." (96:1-2)

"Sing" is mentioned here three times, corresponding to the three times each day when Israel sings praises to God. "Sing unto the Lord," corresponds to the morning (*Shaḥarit*) prayers, when Israel praises God for renewing daily the work of creation. "Sing unto the Lord, all the earth," corresponds to the afternoon (*Minḥah*) prayers, for all of earth's inhabitants have by then enjoyed the sun and its warmth. "Sing unto the Lord, bless His name," alludes to the evening (*Maariv*) prayers, when Israel praises God for bringing on the evening twilight.

Midrash Tehillim 96:1

Adonai malakh tagel ha-aretz ה׳ מָלָךְ תָּגֵל הָאָרֶץ

"The Lord reigneth; let the earth rejoice" (Psalm 97)

COMMENTS ON THE TEXT

"The Lord reigneth; let the earth rejoice;
Let the multitude of isles be glad." (97:1)

Here the psalmist summons the nations to recognize the universal import of God's protection of His people. The deliverance of Israel testifies to the power of God and to His Kingship over all the world. When Israel was delivered from a foe, "The heavens declared His righteousness, and all the peoples saw His glory" (97:6). God Himself, as it were, led His people in battle.

"Clouds and darkness are round about Him;
Righteousness and justice are the foundation of His throne.
A fire goeth before Him,
And burneth up His adversaries round about . . . .
The mountains melted like wax at the presence of the Lord,
At the presence of the Lord of the whole earth." (97:2-5)

The God of Israel is "The Lord of the whole earth." All the forces of nature are mobilized by Him in behalf of His people. He champions their cause because, "righteousness and justice are the foundation of His throne" (97:2).

A similar note is struck in a psalm attributed to David, in which he celebrated his triumph over his adversaries:

The Lord also thundered in the heavens,
And the Most High gave forth His voice;
Hailstones and coals of fire.
And He sent out His arrows and scattered them;
And He shot forth His lightnings, and discomfited them.

Psalms 18:14-15; cf. II Samuel 22:14-15

"O ye that love the Lord, hate evil." (97:10)

A recurring theme in Scripture is that evildoers are the enemies of God, even as the righteous are His friends. A familiar verse conveys this concept: "The Lord preserveth all them that love Him, but all the wicked will He destroy" (Psalms 145:20). Another passage of the same tenor is:

For lo, Thine enemies, O Lord,
For lo, Thine enemies shall perish;
All workers of iniquity shall be scattered. (Psalms 92:10)

In the light of this juxtaposition we can understand the emphatic language of the psalmist as he avows that he is always against those who are God's enemies because they defy His moral law and thus oppose Him.

Do I not hate them, O Lord, that hate Thee?
Do I not strive with those that rise up against Thee?
I hate them with utmost hatred;
I count them mine enemies. (Psalms 139:21-22)

"Light is sown for the righteous." (97:11)

The Septuagint reads here *Zarah* instead of *Zarua* and renders the verse, "Light dawns for the righteous."

SELECTED RABBINIC COMMENTS

"Light is sown for the righteous." (97:11)

Rabbi Abin the Levite said, "When a man constructs windows for himself, he builds them wide on the inside and narrow on the outside so that they might draw in the light and diffuse it in the house. But such was not the case with the windows of the Temple. They were built wide on the outside and narrow on the inside, so that the light which emanated from the Temple could be diffused throughout the world."

Tanḥuma, Tezaveh 6

If the Temple has its own light, why does the Torah say, "Command the Israelites to bring you pure oil of beaten olives for lighting" (Exodus 27:20)? God bids us kindle lights in the Temple so that we might become meritorious by observing the *Mitzvah* of kindling the lights. David said, "Light is sown *for* the righteous," *i.e.*, for the benefit of the righteous.

Tanḥuma, Tezaveh 6

God sowed the light of the Torah and the *Mitzvot* so that everyone in Israel might be deserving of the world to come through having hallowed every mundane activity. No activity in the world is without an accompanying *Mitzvah:* when we plow, we obey the command not to plow with an ox and donkey together (Deuteronomy 22:10); when we sow, we obey the command not to sow a vineyard with mixed seeds (*ibid.* 22:9); and when we reap and forget a sheaf, we obey the command to leave it for the stranger, the fatherless, and the widow (*ibid.* 24:20).

In kneading dough, one must set aside a portion as a gift for the Lord (Numbers 15:20). When an animal is slaughtered, certain parts must be given to the priest (Deuteronomy 18:3). When one chances on a nest, he must not take the mother with the young; he must let the mother bird go (*ibid.* 22:6-7). When one has hunted down an animal or bird that may be eaten, one must pour out the blood and cover it with earth (Leviticus 17:13). When one plants a tree, the fruit of the first three years are forbidden (*ibid.* 19:23). When one has buried his dead, one must obey the admonition, "You are the children of the Lord your God. You shall not gash yourselves or shave the front of your heads because of the dead" (Deuteronomy 14:1). In cutting one's hair, one must not round off the side-growth of the head (Leviticus 19:27). When one builds a house, one must make a parapet for the roof so that no one might fall from there (Deuteronomy 22:8). On the door one must affix a *Mezuzah* (*ibid.* 6:9). When one wears a four-cornered garment one must put fringes on the corners (Numbers 15:38).

Tanḥuma, Shelaḥ 15

Shiru ladonai shir ḥadash שִׁירוּ לַה' שִׁיר חָדָשׁ

"O sing unto the Lord a new song" (Psalm 98)

COMMENTS ON THE TEXT

"He hath remembered His mercy and faithfulness toward the house of Israel;
All the ends of the earth have seen the salvation of our God." (98:3)

As in Psalms 97:1, the psalmist celebrates God's protection of His people which has significance for all peoples (see p. 39).

"Before the Lord, for He is come to judge the earth." (98:9)

Yehezkel Kaufmann's exposition of the *Kabbalat Shabbat* psalms, which has been discussed in the Introduction, argues that God's judgment of the earth is not in a future millennial era but in the present.

SELECTED RABBINIC COMMENTS

"Sing unto the Lord a new song." (98:1)

In the future Israel will sing a song of triumph, for Scripture says, "Sing unto the Lord a new song, for He hath done marvelous things." By what merit shall Israel sing such a song? By the merit of Abraham who unwaveringly trusted in God (Genesis 15:6). It is the same constancy that Israel inherits and of which Scripture says, "But the righteous shall live by his faith" (Habakkuk 2:4).

Exodus Rabbah 23:5

"For He hath done marvelous things." (98:1)

Many things hast Thou done, O Lord my God,
Even Thy wondrous works and Thy thoughts
toward us. (Psalms 40:6)

Every day God performs many wondrous things for us and only He knows about them. Rabbi Elazar ben Pedat said, "Scripture first bids us render praise to 'Him who alone does great wonders' (Psalms 136:4), and following this we are called upon to praise 'Him who divided the Sea of Reeds' (136:13), and later we praise 'Him who giveth food to all flesh' (136:25). Our daily sustenance is thus deemed to be a miracle as marvelous as the cleaving of the Sea. Furthermore, no person goes through life without wonders being performed for him, though he is never aware of them. For example, a man may be lying in bed, with a snake on the ground below him. As the man is about to get up, the snake sees this and glides away. Thus only God knows how many wondrous things He does for each of us every day."

Midrash Tehillim 106:1

"His right hand and His holy arm,
Have wrought salvation [deliverance] for Him." (98:1)

Rabbi Aḥa said, "So long as Israel is in exile, the right hand of God is, as it were, not free. But when Israel is redeemed, Scripture says: 'His right hand and His holy arm have wrought deliverance for Him.' This is what is meant by the prophet, 'The Lord hath made bare His holy arm in the eyes of all the nations; and all the ends of the earth shall see the salvation [deliverance] of our God' (Isaiah 52:10)."

Midrash Tehillim 98:1

"Shout unto the Lord all the earth . . .
Sing praises unto the Lord with the harp . . .
With trumpets and sound of the horn . . .
Let the sea roar, and the fullness thereof . . . ." (98:4-8)

All this rejoicing will be on account of the redemption of Israel. Thus, there cannot be complete rejoicing for mankind until Israel is redeemed.

Midrash Tehillim 98:1

Adonai malakh yirgezu amim ה' מָלָךְ יִרְגְּזוּ עַמִּים

"The Lord reigneth, let the peoples tremble" (Psalm 99)

COMMENTS ON THE TEXT

"He [that] is enthroned upon the cherubim." (99:1)

In many passages Scripture speaks of God as, "The Lord of hosts who is enthroned upon the cherubim" (I Samuel 4:4; II Samuel 6:2; Psalms 80:2, and elsewhere). The wings of the cherubim in Solomon's Temple are described as "spread forth . . . over the place of the ark and the cherubim covered the ark and the staves thereof above [it]" (I Kings 8:7; cf. Exodus 25:19). When King Hezekiah prayed, he addressed God in these words: "O Lord, God of Israel, that is enthroned upon the cherubim, Thou art the God, even Thou alone, of all the kingdoms of the earth" (II Kings 19:15).

The cherubim symbolize the earthly throne of God, and the ark below the cherubim symbolizes His footstool. Thus, the psalmist says, "Exalt ye the Lord . . . and prostrate yourselves at His footstool" (99:5). In a majestic passage in the last chapter of Isaiah, the prophet warns against the tendency to look *at* these symbols, rather than *through* them, thus failing to grasp their exalted meaning.

Thus saith the Lord:
"The heaven is My throne,
And the earth is My footstool;
Where is the house that you may build unto Me?
And where is the place that may be My resting place?
For all these things [*i.e.*, heaven and earth]
My hand hath made
And so all these things came to be,
Saith the Lord;
But [only] on this man will I look,
Even on him that is poor and of a contrite spirit,
And trembleth at My word." (Isaiah 66:1-2)

"Moses and Aaron among His priests,
And Samuel among them that call upon His name." (99:6)

Moses, Aaron, and Samuel served their people in critical periods in the history of Israel and a mere reference to them was enough to awaken collective memories of deep admiration and profound reverence. Moses and Aaron led the Israelites in the liberation from Egyptian bondage and both ministered to them during the forty years of wandering in the Sinai desert.

Moses and Samuel were also paired together by Jeremiah. He chided his contemporaries for straying so far away from God that, "Though Moses and Samuel stood before Me, yet My mind could not be toward this people; cast them out of My sight and let them go" (Jeremiah 15:1). Samuel guided the people during the time of the establishment of the monarchy under Saul, whom he anointed as the first king of Israel (I Samuel 10:1). When Saul incurred Samuel's displeasure, he anointed David as his eventual successor (*ibid.* 16:13-14). Moses and Samuel are here set up as prophets rather than as political leaders. They are depicted as having successfully implored God for their people and as having transmitted to the people the terms of God's covenant with Israel, which was so impressively enacted under the direction of Moses and Aaron. When the record of the covenant was first read aloud to the people they accepted its terms with the declaration, "All that the Lord has spoken we will faithfully do" (Exodus 24:7). Samuel is also paired with David in appointing the Levites for various duties in the Tabernacle in Jerusalem (I Chronicles 9:22).

"Thou wast a forgiving God . . .
Though punishing them for their misdeeds." (99:8)

The notion that God is at once forgiving and yet exacting in His retribution for misdeeds is more explicitly expressed in this verse:

> The Lord, the Lord, a God compassionate and gracious, slow to anger, rich in steadfast kindness, extending kindness to the thousandth generation, forgiving iniquity, transgression, and

sin; yet He does not remit all punishment, but visits the iniquity of fathers upon children and children's children, upon the third and fourth generations. (Exodus 34:6-8)

SELECTED RABBINIC COMMENTS

"The Lord is great in Zion." (99:2)

Rabbi Levi said, "All the blessings, bounties, and comforts which God will in the future confer on Israel will go forth from Zion:

Torah: 'For out of Zion shall go forth Torah.' (Isaiah 2:3)

God's blessing: 'The Lord bless thee out of Zion.' (Psalms 128:5)

God's shining forth: 'Out of Zion, the perfection of beauty, God hath shined forth.' (Psalms 50:2)

Strength: 'The Lord strengthen thee out of Zion.' (Psalms 20:2)

Life: 'Like the dew of Hermon, that cometh down upon the mountains of Zion, for there the Lord commanded the blessing, even life for ever and ever.' (Psalms 133:2)

Greatness: 'The Lord is great in Zion.' (Psalms 99:2)

Deliverance: 'Oh that the salvation [deliverance] of Israel were come out of Zion.' (Psalms 14:7)"

Midrash Tehillim 14:6, abridged;
cf. Leviticus Rabbah 24:4; Pesikta Rabbati 4:1

"Thou hast established equity." (99:4)

Rabbi Alexandre said, "This means that God has established harmony in His world [through the laws of the Torah]. When a man has a claim against his fellow and he appears before the court with him, after they both have accepted the law's decision, they make peace. This is what is meant by the verse, 'Thou hast established equity.'

"Another example: when a man sees his enemy's animal prostrate under its burden, he gives him a hand and helps his enemy unload the animal and then helps him to load it again, then they go together into an inn. The owner of the animal says to himself, 'That fellow is really my friend and here I thought that he was my enemy.' There and then they converse with one another, with the result that peace is established between them. What caused them to make peace and become friends? It was that the first man kept what is written in the Torah: 'When you see the animal of your enemy prostrate under its burden and would refrain from raising it, you must nevertheless raise it with him' (Exodus 23:5). This confirms what is written in Scripture, 'Her [the Torah's] ways are ways of pleasantness and all her paths are peace' (Proverbs 3:17)."

Midrash Tehillim 99:3

"Moses and Aaron among His priests,
And Samuel among them that call upon His name." (99:6)

Solomon said, "A worker's sleep is sweet whether he eats much or little" (Ecclesiastes 5:11). They said to Solomon, "It is not really so. When a man is hungry and he eats only a little, he is restless and cannot sleep but when he eats plenty, his sleep is sweet!" He replied to them, "I was only talking about the reward of the righteous who toil in the Torah. For example, take the case of a man who lived only thirty years, but who from age ten on toiled in the study of Torah and the practice of *Mitzvot,* while another man lived eighty years and until his dying day, he toiled in the study of Torah and the practice of *Mitzvot*. One might think that since the first man toiled only thirty years and the other man toiled eighty years, God rewards the second more than the first. Therefore, I [Solomon] say that whether a man eats much or little [of the Torah's nourishment], the reward is the same. For the man who died at age thirty, could say to God, 'Had You not taken me away so early in life, I would have had to my credit much more

Torah and *Mitzvot.*' Thus, the reward of one is as great as the reward of the other.'' Said Rabbi Tanḥu, ''You can see that this is so from the fact that Moses served Israel in Egypt and in the desert for forty years and died at the age of one hundred twenty, while Samuel died at an early age of fifty-two. However, because Samuel bore the burden and the bother of Israel, Scripture equates him with Moses and Aaron regardless of his brief lifespan of fifty-two years.''

Tanḥuma, Ki Tissa 3

Moses chose seventy elders to help him govern the people in the desert (Numbers 11:16-17). Why are the names of those elders not mentioned? The reason is that in the future a man might say, ''So and So is like Nadab and Abihu [Aaron's sons] and So and So is like Eldad and Medad'' (Numbers 11:26-29). But Scripture does not use such comparisons. It says, ''It is the Lord that made Moses and Aaron'' (I Samuel 12:6) and then it goes on to say, ''And the Lord sent Jerubbaal and Bedan and Jephthah and Samuel'' (I Samuel 12:11). Scripture also says, ''Moses and Aaron among His priests, and Samuel among them that call upon His name'' (Psalms 99:6). Thus, Scripture puts three of the least important leaders on the same level with three of the most distinguished leaders. This serves to teach us that Jerubbaal was as important in his generation as Moses was in his generation, and that Bedan was as important in his generation as Aaron was in his generation, and that Jephthah was as important in his generation as Samuel was in his generation. Even when a not very eminent person is appointed leader of his community, he is to be respected as the noblest of the noble. Scripture also says, ''You shall appear before the Levitical priests or the magistrates in charge at that time'' (Deuteronomy 17:9). Would it ever occur to you to go to a magistrate who is not of your time? Evidently the point is that you must look to the leader of your own time, bearing in mind the verse, ''Don't say: 'How is it that the former times are better than these?' For it is not wise of you to ask that question'' (Ecclesiastes 7:10).

Talmud, Rosh Hashanah 25a-b

Havu ladonai b'nei elim הָבוּ לַה' בְּנֵי אֵלִים

"Ascribe unto the Lord, O ye sons of might" (Psalm 29)

COMMENTS ON THE TEXT

The Septuagint translation of this psalm has the superscription: "For the *Atzeret* of Sukkot." H. L. Ginsberg explained that the original reading of the superscription was *"Atzeret,"* and in Rabbinic Hebrew *Atzeret* means *Shavuot,* a holiday which occurs exactly seven weeks after Passover and is therefore the *Atzeret* (solemn assembly) of Shavuot. The Rabbis saw in the "voice of the Lord," (29:3) allusions to the giving of the Torah at Sinai. Ginsberg surmised that there must have been a Hebrew manuscript with the superscription, "For *Atzeret,"* and that some scribe, unfamiliar with Rabbinic Hebrew and thinking that it refers to *Shemini Atzeret,* mistakenly added the words, "of Sukkot."

"Sons of might [divine beings]." (29:1)

The Hebrew *B'nei Elim,* means literally, "sons of gods," *i.e.,* the divine beings who are the celestial retinue of God and who obey Him (Psalms 103:21). Here the denizens of the heavenly regions are summoned to offer Him tributes of glory and majesty. But in Psalms 96:7 all mankind is called on to render praise to God: "Ascribe unto the Lord, ye kindreds of the peoples, ascribe unto the Lord glory and majesty."

"The wilderness of Kadesh." (29:8)

Ginsberg pointed out that the thunderstorm moved from west to east and that the "wilderness of Kadesh" is a phrase also used in Ugaritic so that it is not to be identified with the Kadesh of the wilderness of Sinai, which was south of Canaan (Numbers 20:16).

"Maketh the hinds to calve." (29:9)

The terrifying storm makes them give birth prematurely.

"And strippeth the forests bare." (29:9)

Ginsberg suggested that *Yearot* which is rendered here as "forests," may mean some type of desert animal which was so terror stricken by the storm that it too gave birth prematurely. He adds that in Arabic, the word *Ḥasaf,* rendered here as "strippeth bare," points to the meaning "quick birth."

"And in His temple all say, 'Glory.' " (29:9)

On earth the thunder and lightning demonstrate the awesome power of God, and in the heavens above all proclaim His glory (Ginsberg).

"God sat enthroned at the flood." (29:10)

Ginsberg commented that this refers to the upper waters mentioned in the verse, "Who layest the beams of Thine upper chambers in the waters" (Psalms 104:3).

A previously mentioned, this psalm is associated with the giving of the Torah because, like the Pentateuch, it mentions the word *Kol* (voice) seven times (see the Introduction, p. 29).

SELECTED RABBINIC COMMENTS

"Ascribe unto the Lord, O ye sons of might [divine beings], Ascribe unto the Lord glory and majesty." (29:1)

With a slight change of vocalization, *B'nei Elim* (divine beings) can be read, *B'nei Illem (Illmim),* which means "mute sons." The people of Israel have a right to remonstrate with God regarding their bitter plight but instead they keep silent like mutes. Furthermore, they suffer under the yoke of the nations in order to hallow His name, unquestionably accepting His severe decrees. Abraham set the example for his descendants. He said, "I could have argued with God in this way: First you assure me, 'Through Isaac, offspring shall be continued for you' (Genesis 21:12), and now You say, 'Take your son, your favored one, Isaac, whom you love, and . . . offer him as a burnt offering' (*ibid.* 22:2). I could have also said: 'You promised that You would maintain Your covenant with Isaac' (*ibid.* 17:7)—what about that covenant? But I kept silent and did not talk. Therefore, when my descendants are entrapped in sin, invoke my silence in their behalf and forgive them." Hence it is written, "Ascribe unto the Lord, O ye sons, who act as if you were mutes."

Midrash Tehillim 29:1

Reflection

Our religious faith is shaken and we are sorely perplexed whenever we reflect on human sufferings for which no rational explanation is available. Rather than declare that there is, "neither Judge nor justice" in the world, the man of firm faith responds with Job, "Though He slay me, yet will I trust in Him" (Job 13:15). Such an unquestioning trust in God is reflected in the statement attributed to Rabbi Levi Yitzḥak of Berditchev: "I do not ask, Lord of the universe, that You reveal to me the secret of Your ways, for I could never comprehend them. I do not ask *why* I suffer. I only ask this: 'Do I suffer for Your sake?' "

"The voice of the Lord is powerful [*Hebrew:* 'with power']." (29:4)

The voice of the Lord comes not "with His power" but "with power," that is, according to the perceptive power of each person. At Sinai each person heard the divine voice in accordance with his capacity to understand. For in the Ten Commandments God says, "I, the Lord, am thy God [second person]" (Exodus 20:2). Said God to Israel, "Think not that because there were many voices there must be many gods. I am the Lord! I am the same God to each one of you."

Yalkut, Yitro 286

"The voice of the Lord maketh the hinds to calve
And strippeth the forests bare;
And in His temple all say, 'Glory.'

The Lord will give strength to His people;
The Lord will bless His people with peace." (29:9, 11)

When the Torah was about to be given to Israel, a loud voice went forth from one end of the world to the other. All the kings of the heathen nations were stricken with terror in their palaces. They began to sing a song of glory to God, as Scripture says, "And in his palace each [king] says: 'Glory.' " In consternation they gathered around Balaam's house and said, "What means that tumultuous noise that we have heard? Is a new flood about to come upon the world?" "No," he replied, "God swore long ago that He would never bring another flood upon the world." . . . "What then, was the noise that we heard?" He replied. "God has a precious treasure in His storehouse. It has been kept stored up for 974 generations* before the creation of the world. Now He wants to give it to His children, the people of Israel, for it is written, 'The Lord will give strength [Torah] to His people.' " Immediately they all declared: "May the Lord bless His people with peace."

Talmud, Zevaḥim 116a

*Lekhah Dodi*** לְכָה דוֹדִי

"Come, my beloved, to meet the Bride"

Solomon Halevi Alkabez, the mystic who composed this poem into which is built an acrostic of his own name, depicts the Sabbath as a bride that has a weekly tryst with her beloved, the people of Israel. The personification of the Sabbath in Talmud and Midrash and the designation of the Sabbath as Israel's bride (see the Introduction), inspired Solomon Alkabez to compose this

* In Rabbinic tradition, God had originally planned to award the Torah to Israel on the thousandth generation of mankind. But only twenty-six generations can be counted from Adam to Moses who received the Torah. Hence 974 generations elapsed before Creation. The 974 generations added to the 26 generations made the thousand generations mentioned in the verse, "The word which He commanded to a thousand generations" (Psalms 105:8). (Midrash Tehillim 105:3)

** For additional comments on *Lekhah Dodi,* see pp. 17-20.

poem. Several centuries had passed since the canon of the standard prayerbook had virtually been closed, and few new *Piyyutim* were being admitted into the liturgy. An exception is *Lekhah Dodi*. Perhaps the pageantry associated with the poem, the Talmudic background of its refrain "Come, my beloved, to meet the Bride," and the boundless popular affection and reverence for the Sabbath, added to the author's acquaintance with Joseph Karo, the author of the *Shulḥan Arukh*, accounts for *Lekhah Dodi's* admission into the liturgy.

When the last stanza, *Bo-i ve-Shalom*, is recited, many congregations rise and face toward the door as if to acknowledge the arrival of a welcome guest, the Sabbath Bride and Queen.

Midrashic and Biblical allusions in *Lekhah Dodi*

"*Shamor* and *Zakhor* were spoken simultaneously."

Shamor is the first word of the fourth commandment in Deuteronomy 5:12, while *Zakhor* is the first word of the same commandment in Exodus 20:8. The author mentions the Deuteronomy version first because he has constructed the poem as an acrostic of his name *Shelomo ha-Levi*. The Rabbis fancifully explain the discrepancy between the two versions by stating that God uttered both words simultaneously.

Mekhilta, ed. Horowitz-Rabin, p. 229

"For it [the Sabbath] is a source of blessing."

When God ordained and hallowed the Sabbath, life was enriched with relaxation, repose, serenity of mind, and quiet contemplation.

Genesis Rabbah 10:9

"Let us go to greet the Sabbath."

See the Introduction on the Kabbalists' practice of going out into the fields to welcome the Sabbath.

"Of old, in ancient times fashioned."

The Torah was in God's treasury 974 generations before the world was created and the Sabbath which is ordained in it was thus fashioned before the world was created. See the Selected Rabbinic Comments for Psalm 29, p. 52.

Talmud, Zevaḥim 116a

"Last in creation but first in conception."

That the Sabbath was in the thought of God before Creation, is the import of a Talmudic parable which compares the creation of the world to an earthly king's construction of a bridal chamber. The king plastered it and panelled it and painted it. Now that the bridal canopy was ready, only one thing was missing, the bride. That king surely must have had in mind a particular bride before the canopy was built. Likewise, when God finished the beautiful world with its planets and stars, with its vegetation and animals, and with man who is the crown of creation, only one thing was still missing and that was the Sabbath Bride. Therefore, on the seventh day, He rested and thus the Sabbath appeared. It surely must have been in the mind of God long before Creation.

Genesis Rabbah 10:9

"O royal sanctuary, seat of God's kingdom,
rise from your ruins."

The inspiration for this and the other references to the redemption may have been the Talmudic assertion that the Sabbath is so important that were the entire people of Israel to observe just two Sabbaths in perfect fashion, the exile would come to an end. (See p. 37.)

Talmud, Shabbat 118b

"The valley of Baca."

This phrase is inspired by the verse, "Passing through the valley of Baca [taken to mean "weeping"] they make it a place of springs" (Psalms 84:7).

"The song of Jesse the Bethlehemite."

A reference to the Messiah who is to be a descendant of David, son of Jesse, of the town of Bethlehem (I Samuel 17:12).

"The glory of the Lord."

These phrases are inspired by the verse, "Arise, shine, for thy light is come, the glory of the Lord is risen upon thee" (Isaiah 60:1).

"Thy God shall rejoice over thee."

This stems from, "As the bridegroom rejoices over the bride, so shall thy God rejoice over thee" (Isaiah 62:5).

"By a man, son of Perez."

An allusion to the Messiah who is to be a descendant of David whose lineage, as given in Ruth 4:18-22, begins with Perez.

"The treasured people."

Suggested to the author by the verse, "You shall be My treasured possession among all the peoples" (Exodus 19:5).

Consoling the mourners

On the first Sabbath eve after the funeral, the mourners, who stay home for *Shivah* (the seven days of mourning), enter the synagogue and are greeted with the words: "May God comfort you among the other mourners for Zion and Jerusalem."

On festival nights

When a festival or one of its intermediate days occurs on a Sabbath, the six *Kabbalat Shabbat* psalms (which symbolize the six workdays of the week) and *Lekhah Dodi* are omitted; instead the service begins with the Sabbath Psalm (Psalm 92).

In *Nusaḥ Sefard* (a modified version of the Ashkenazi liturgy), only Psalms 95-99 are omitted and the service begins with Psalm 29, which is followed by the chanting of a "shortened" version of *Lekhah Dodi* (the first and last two stanzas).

Mizmor shir le-yom ha-Shabbat מִזְמוֹר שִׁיר לְיוֹם הַשַּׁבָּת

"A Psalm. A Song. For the Sabbath day" (Psalm 92)

The rubric of this psalm indicates that it was recited on the Sabbath day. The Mishnah informs us that on each day of the week, a designated psalm was recited by the Levites in connection with the daily *Tamid* offering, and it identifies these psalms (Mishnah, Tamid 7:4). The same psalms are included in the Prayer Book for recitation during the corresponding daily morning services. In the Hebrew text of the "daily" psalms only the Sabbath psalm has a rubric, but in the Septuagint translation each of the "daily" psalms has a superscription which indicates the day on which it was recited.

One would be hard put to delineate in the texts and contexts of these psalms a clear association with the days for which they were designated.* Rabbi Akiva, with his singular method of Biblical interpretation, saw in the first six psalms a rehearsal of the drama of Creation and a tribute to the Creator. However, in the psalm for the Sabbath, he perceived a portrayal of the future bliss and felicity in an era that is to be "wholly Sabbath" (Talmud, Rosh Hashanah 31a). Indeed, the grace after Sabbath meals (*Birkat ha-Mazon*) contains a supplication, "May the Merciful One give us as our heritage a day which is wholly Sabbath and rest in eternal life."

In the light of Rabbi Akiva's characterization of the Sabbath psalm, which accounts for its recital on the Sabbath day, we can understand and appreciate the Midrashic statement that man's earthly life is to be regarded as the eve of a blissful celestial life when, by meticulous observance of the Sabbath, spiritual preparation is to be made for a "wholly Sabbath" time of eternity.

Nahum Sarna** sees the Creation motif as the dominant theme of this psalm. He avows that the superscription is descriptive as well as liturgical in nature and that the Biblical account of Creation

---

* An interesting analysis is offered by L. J. Liebreich in *Eretz-Israel,* Vol. III, pp. 170-173.

** "The Psalm for the Sabbath Day," *Journal of Biblical Literature,* LXXXI (1962), pp. 155-168.

controls the imagery and influences the language and style of the psalm. The punishment of the wicked and the triumph of the righteous about which the psalm speaks reflect "the mythical conflict of God with the rebellious forces of primeval chaos." Sarna cites striking parallels from Ugaritic and other Near East as well as Biblical texts. In addition, he draws attention to the fact that, like Psalm 29, this psalm also mentions the Tetragrammaton (*Adonai*) seven times, making it all the more suitable for the Sabbath day (Palestinian Talmud, Taanit 65c).

Despite the cosmic scale on which Sarna assesses this psalm, it is more plausible, if less ambitious, to regard its origin as a prayer of gratitude by an individual who had been delivered from the evil designs of his enemies. After his escape from their vicious plot, he goes to the Temple to express his gratitude:

> For Thou, O Lord, hast made me glad through Thy work;
> I will exult in the works of Thy hands. (92:5)

Borne on the crest of a wave of triumph and enthusiasm, the psalmist sees in his deliverance a paradigm of God's government of the world. The wicked, being untutored and foolish, do not understand God's purposes. Otherwise they would understand that their prosperity is ephemeral and that it is only a prelude to their inevitable doom (92:7-8). On the other hand, the righteous are firmly rooted and they can face the future with confidence. Indeed, they will live to a ripe old age in close proximity to the Temple and they will tell others that God's ways are just and flawless (92:13-15).

The finality with which this psalmist expresses himself, derives from the exuberance of a heart suffused with the sense of the accessibility to God. His fervent faith was born out of a particular experience that makes him quite oblivious of the innocent suffering that many blameless people have to endure. A more penetrating analysis of the problem of innocent suffering is offered by the author of Psalm 73. He was agitated by the same question that Jeremiah worded so succinctly: "Why does the way of the wicked prosper?" (Jeremiah 12:1). This psalmist came to the conclusion that the accessibility and nearness of God was to him a tower of strength when his own strength failed.

Whom have I in heaven but Thee?
And besides Thee I desire none upon earth.
My flesh and my heart faileth;
But God is the rock of my heart
And my portion for ever.
For lo, they that go far from Thee shall perish; . . .
But as for me, the nearness of God
is my good. . . . (Psalms 73:25-28)

Still another psalmist, from the abyss of his own anguish and the suffering of his people, offers this bold and uninhibited complaint:

Awake, why sleepest Thou, O Lord?
Arouse Thyself, cast [us] not off forever.
Wherefore hidest Thou Thy face,
And forgettest our affliction and our oppression?
(Psalms 44:24-25)

The entire Book of Job wrestles with the baffling problem of human suffering and it finally arrives at a conclusion so tersely formulated by Rabbi Yannai:

"It is not in our power to explain either the prosperity of the wicked or the sufferings of the righteous" (Mishnah, Avot 4:15). The Book of Job implies that man will have to learn to be courageously virtuous in face of the elusiveness and inequity of reward and punishment for his moral conduct.

The psalms, dealing with the problem of evil in a world governed by a compassionate God, do not offer a definitive explanation of the human predicament but they are suffused with a firm conviction of the certainty of God's existence and of His accessibility to man. That certainty is expressed with compelling freshness in these words:

Whither shall I go from Thy spirit?
Or whither shall I flee from Thy presence?
If I ascend up into heaven, Thou art there;
If I make my bed in the nether-world, Thou art there.
If I take the wings of the morning,

And dwell in the uttermost parts of the sea;
Even there would Thy hand lead me,
And Thy right hand would hold me. (Psalms 139:7-10)

Kohelet characterized the human situation with its cyclic circumstances and contrasting vicissitudes, in this passage:

A season is set for everything,
A time for every experience under heaven:
A time for weeping and a time for laughing,
A time for wailing and a time for dancing.
(Ecclesiastes 3:1, 4)

The implication can be drawn here that one must not borrow trouble from the future. This sagacious advice is also conveyed by the following Midrashic tale:

> A pagan asked Rabbi Joshua ben Korḥa: "Don't you believe that God sees the future?" "Yes," he answered. "Then why does the Torah say: 'And the Lord regretted that He had made man on earth, and His heart was saddened?' " (Genesis 6:6). In reply, Rabbi Joshua asked him, "Have you ever had a son born to you?" "Yes" the pagan answered. "What did you do when he was born?" "I was happy and I invited others to share my happiness." "Didn't you know then that your son would some day die?" "In a time of happiness," the pagan said, "one should be happy and in a time of mourning one should be sad."
>
> *Genesis Rabbah 27:4*

The author of Psalm 92 experienced a great deliverance, and, in the incandescent words of this psalm, he expressed the grateful and jubilant feeling that welled up in his heart.

COMMENTS ON THE TEXT

"To declare Thy lovingkindness in the morning,
And Thy faithfulness in the night seasons." (92:3)

The word *Emunah,* here rendered "faithfulness," should be

more correctly rendered "goodness," as in Psalms 36:6, 89:25, Lamentations 3:23, and in other Biblical passages.

Here the sense is, "to tell of God's lovingkindness and goodness in the mornings and at night-times" (H. L. Ginsberg).

"For lo, Thine enemies, O Lord,
For lo, Thine enemies shall perish." (92:10)

On the concept that evildoers are enemies of God, see the comment on Psalms 97:10.

"Mine eye also has gazed on them that lie in wait for me." (92:12)

That is, I witnessed their downfall.

"Mine ears have heard my desire . . ." (92:12)

This means, "I heard of the troubles into which they fell."

"My Rock, in whom there is no unrighteousness." (92:16)

The emendation of *Tzuri* to *Tzaddik* yields, "He is a Righteous One, in whom there is no unrighteousness" (cf. Deuteronomy 32:4). (H.L. Ginsberg)

SELECTED RABBINIC COMMENTS

"A Psalm. A Song. For the Sabbath day." (92:1)

God said, "I created seven firmaments, and of all of them I chose as My abode only the skies [*Arabot*], as Scripture says, 'Extol Him that rideth upon the skies' (Psalms 68:5). I created seven lands, and out of all of them I chose none other than *Eretz Yisrael,* as Scripture says, 'It is a land which the Lord your God looks after, on which the Lord your God always keeps His eye, from year's beginning to year's end' (Deuteronomy 11:12)." God created seven mountains and out of all of them He chose only Mount Sinai, as Scripture says, "The mountain which God hath desired as His abode'' (Psalms 68:17). God said, ''I created seven seas and of all of them I chose the Sea of Kinnereth [*i.e.*, the Sea of Galilee] and gave it to the tribe of Naphtali as a possession, as Scripture says, 'O Naphtali, sated with favor and full of the Lord's blessing, take possession on the west* and south' (Deuteronomy 33:23). I created seven worlds and of all of them I chose only the seventh, six of them being destined to come and the seventh being the one which will be wholly Sabbath and rest in eternal life.** I created seven days and of all of them I chose only the seventh day, as Scripture says, 'And God blessed the seventh day' (Genesis 2:3). I created seven years and of them I chose only the seventh year of remission, as Scripture says, 'Every seventh year you shall practice remission of debts' (Deuteronomy 15:1).''

Midrash Tehillim 92:2

Whoever keeps the Sabbath, his sins are pardoned by the Holy One, blessed be He, for the prophet says, ''Happy is the man . . . that keeps the Sabbath from profaning it'' (Isaiah 56:2). The word for *''profaning'' (Meḥallelo)* can be read as ''he is pardoned'' *(Maḥul Lo)*.

Midrash Tehillim 92:2

We are commanded, ''Remember the Sabbath day and keep it holy'' (Exodus 20:8), and we are told by the prophet, ''Call the Sabbath 'Delight' and the holy [day] of the Lord 'Honored One' '' (Isaiah 58:13). The people of Israel honor the Sabbath with food, drink, and clean garments. Moreover, they welcome it with psalmody and song, as Scripture says, ''A Psalm. A Song. For the Sabbath day.''

Midrash Tehillim 92:3

"It is good to give thanks unto the Lord." (92:2)

In a Midrashic flight of the imagination, Psalm 92 was ascribed to the joint authorship of Adam and the Sabbath itself. Rabbi Levi said, ''When Adam disobeyed God's command, He sat

* *Yam* ''west'' can also be rendered ''sea.''

** See the introductory comment on Psalm 92, p. 56.

in judgment over him in order to punish him. But this is what happened: Adam was created on the eve of the Sabbath [*i.e.*, Friday]. In the first hour, the thought of creating him entered God's mind; in the second hour, God consulted the ministering angels; in the third, He gathered the dust; in the fourth, He kneaded it; in the fifth hour, He made him into a formless lump; in the sixth, He formed his joints; in the seventh, He blew into him the breath of life; in the eighth, He stood him on his feet; in the ninth, He commanded him; in the tenth, Adam sinned; in the eleventh hour he was expelled, for when He was about to pronounce punishment, the Sabbath arrived and the Sabbath became Adam's advocate. It said to God, 'During the six days of Creation no one was punished. Will You begin with me? Is this my holiness and is this my rest?' Thus through the intervention of the Sabbath, Adam was spared from punishment in Gehenna. Seeing the power of the Sabbath, Adam was about to sing a hymn in its honor. But the Sabbath said to Adam, 'Do you sing a hymn to me? Let us together sing a hymn to the Holy One, blessed be He.' So they both declared, 'It is good to give thanks unto the Lord.' "

Midrash Tehillim 92:1

Another Midrash gives a different account of the occasion that inspired Adam to compose the Sabbath Psalm. Adam met Cain, who told him that after he slew his brother Abel, he repented and thus propitiated God who then reduced the severity of his punishment. Adam then exclaimed, "Such is the power of repentance, and I knew it not!" Thereupon he composed a song of praise to God, beginning with the words, "It is good to *confess* [*Lehodot* can also be rendered "to confess"] your sins unto the Lord." Rabbi Levi said that this psalm of Adam was later forgotten and was restored to liturgical use by Moses.

Genesis Rabbah 22:13

"It is good to give thanks [*Lehodot*] unto the Lord." (92:2)

The word *Lehodot* means "to give thanks" and it also means "to confess." In saying this Adam meant: Through me all future generations will learn that when one confesses his sins and forsakes them, he will be saved from the punishment of Gehenna for, "It is good to 'confess' unto the Lord."

Midrash Tehillim 92:7

"With a solemn sound upon the harp." (92:4)

The Hebrew text is, *Alei Higgayon Bekhinor. Higgayon* means "with utterance" and *Bekhinor* means "with the music of the harp." If *Alei* was vocalized *Alai,* "for Me," the message of the verse would be: The Holy One, blessed be He, said: "I demand from Israel not the music of the harp but the utterance of their mouth, as Scripture says, 'To Me [*Alai*] an utterance in prayer is like the music of the harp.' "

Midrash Tehillim 92:7

"But Thou, O Lord, art on high for evermore." (92:9)

Rabbi Berechiah said in the name of Rabbi Levi: It is written, "Thou, O Lord, art on high for evermore," meaning, "God is always just." When an earthly king sits in judgment, all the people praise him when he acquits the accused, none praise him when he condemns a person to death, for they know that he is prone to pronounce sentence in passion or blindness. But with God it is not so. Whether He remits or punishes, He is always just and right. Rabbi Huna, son of Rabbi Aha, quoted this verse, "I will sing of mercy and justice; unto Thee, O Lord, will I sing praises" (Psalms 101:1). David said, "Be it one way or the other, in weal or in woe, to You, O Lord, will I sing."

Leviticus Rabbah 24:2

"The righteous shall flourish like the palm tree." (92:13)

Rabbi Ada bar Ada said: "As the palm tree casts its shadow far away from it, so the reward of the righteous is far away from them, even as distant as the world to come, as it is written, 'Know therefore that only the Lord your God is God, the steadfast God who keeps His gracious covenant to the thousandth generation of those who love Him and keep His commandments' " (Deuteronomy 7:9).

Midrash Tehillim 92:11

"They shall bring forth fruit in old age." (92:15)

The Hebrew for "bring forth fruit" is *Yenuvun*. This suggests *Nivin* ("teeth") and the verse can thus serve to remind us of a story about Rabbi Joshua ben Korḥa. At the age of one hundred he grew new teeth and even begot a son. But old as he was, Rabbi Joshua ben Korḥa was still being consulted as an expert in difficult legal cases. Once there came before the court the case of a man who had specified in his will that his son should inherit none of his estate till he became a fool. Puzzled about the execution of such a will, Rabbi José and Rabbi Judah (ha-Nasi) went to consult with the venerable and learned Rabbi Joshua ben Korḥa. They spotted him outside in the field, and saw him crawling on his hands and feet, with a reed sticking out of his mouth and being dragged along by his child. Seeing him in this condition, they hid themselves in order not to embarrass him. Later they entered his house and they asked him about the case with the strange provision in that will. He began to laugh and said to them, "As you live, this stipulation that you ask me about could very well be applied to me now. You know that when a man becomes a father and plays with his child he is prone to behave like a fool."

Midrash Tehillim 92:13

"To declare that the Lord is upright." (92:16)

They asked Moses, "Who was responsible for your not entering the Promised Land?" "I myself was responsible," he answered. "Did not the Holy One, blessed be He, do this to you?" they asked. "God forbid," he said. "Even when it seems to us that God is exonerating the wicked and condemning the righteous [we must declare]:

'The Rock—His deeds are perfect,
Yea, all His ways are just;
A faithful God, never false,
True and upright is He.' " (Deuteronomy 32:4)

They asked Adam, "Who brought death on you?" "I brought it on myself," he answered. "Was it not God who did this to you?" "God forbid," said Adam to them. "My situation is like that of a sick man who was confined to his bed. When the physician came and examined him, he proceeded to give him instructions: You may eat such and such food, but you may not eat such and such food, because it will be bad for you and endanger your life. Nevertheless, he ate that [unwholesome] food and became deathly sick. People then asked him, 'Was it possibly the physician who brought this on you?' 'Not at all,' he said. 'I brought this on myself, for, had I obeyed his instructions I would not now be at the brink of death.' So is the case with me," said Adam. "I was told: 'Of every tree of the garden you are free to eat; but as for the tree of knowledge of good and bad, you must not eat of it' (Genesis 2:16-17). I have brought this on myself, and this is what is meant by, 'For the word of the Lord is upright' (Psalms 33:4)."

Midrash Tehillim 92:14

Adonai malakh ge-ut lavesh ה' מָלָךְ גֵּאוּת לָבֵשׁ

"The Lord reigneth; He is clothed in majesty" (Psalm 93)

The psalmist describes his feelings on a stormy day. The rising torrential floods with their thunderous roaring seem to threaten the existence of the world God has created. Throughout these convulsive phenomena, he remains unafraid for, "the Lord reigns" (93:1). It is God's majesty and power that assure the stability and endurance of the world which cannot be moved because His throne is established from time immemorial (93:2). There follows a vague reference to a primordial struggle in which the Creator asserts His power over brute nature (93:3). But, "above the voices of the many waters, the mighty breakers of the sea, the Lord on high is mighty (93:4). The concluding verse, "Thy testimonies are very sure" (93:5) follows the pattern of Psalm 19, which begins with the celebration of God as Sovereign over the natural order and concludes with praise of the moral order prescribed by the Torah through which destructive human passions are kept in check:

> Thy testimonies [laws] are very sure,
> Holiness becometh Thy House,
> O Lord, for evermore. (93:5)

The Septuagint has a superscription to this psalm to the effect that it was recited on the sixth day of the week. Indeed, the Mishnah informs us that the psalm was sung by the Levites on Friday as the prescribed morning sacrifice was being offered on the altar in the Temple (Tamid 7:4). Rabbi Akiva explained that on the sixth day of the week God completed the creation of all that exists and all that lives. It was then that He proclaimed His Kingship over the universe (Talmud, Rosh Hashanah 31a).

SELECTED RABBINIC COMMENTS

"Thy throne is established of old." (93:2)

God's throne is one of the six things which He had in mind before He created the world. They are: (1) The Throne of Glory, (2) Messiah, (3) The Torah, (4) Israel, (5) The Temple, and (6) Repentance.

Midrash Tehillim 93:3

"The floods have lifted up, O Lord,
The floods have lifted up their voice." (93:3)

Rabbi Berechiah offered this parable in the name of Rabbi Abba bar Kahana: A king built a palace and had it inhabited entirely by deaf mutes. Though they could not express their gratitude in words, they did express it by signs and gestures. Not a day would pass without a solicitous inquiry after the health of their royal benefactor. The king was deeply touched by their mute expressions of loyalty, and he reasoned that if he could fill that palace with inhabitants possessed of the power of speech, they would thank him in language of enduring beauty. So he peopled the palace with those able to express themselves in speech. Almost immediately the new occupants seized the palace and announced, "This palace now belongs to us and not to the king." Whereupon the king decreed that the rebels be ejected and the mutes be brought back to the palace.

When God created the world, the roaring waters praised Him, as Scripture tells us: "The floods have lifted up, O Lord, . . . the floods have lifted up their roaring" (Psalms 93:3). And what did the waters say? "Mighty on high is the Lord" (Psalms 93:4). Said God: "If the floods, which have not the faculty of speech, declare My glory so fervently, how much more would articulate man express gratitude to his Creator?" So He created man, a being endowed with speech. But what happened? Generation followed upon generation and each repudiated God's rule. So what did He do? He said, "Let these rebels be cleared out and let the mute servants return!" Whereupon He brought a flood on a corrupt humanity.

Genesis Rabbah 5:1

"Thy testimonies are very sure,
Holiness becometh Thy House,
O Lord, for evermore." (93:5)

Moses [to whom the authorship of this psalm is also attributed,] said to God, "O Master of the universe, when You weaken the voice of the Torah and the voice of the Temple, You make louder the voice of the wicked nations. But when You make louder the voice of the Torah and the voice of the Temple, You weaken the voice of the wicked nations." Therefore, "May Your House be rebuilt on permanent foundations" [unlike the first and second Temples which were destroyed through Israel's neglect of the Torah].

Midrash Tehillim 93:8

The Kaddish קַדִּישׁ

"Magnified and sanctified be His great name"

In some congregations, mourners recite the *Kaddish* at this point in the service after Psalms 92 and 93 have been recited. The eighth-century Tractate Soferim (10:7) includes the *Kaddish* among the prayers for which the presence of a *Minyan* is required.

The *Kaddish* is a magnificent affirmation of Judaism's hope that the Kingship of God, which Israel proclaims and under which it orders its life, may be extended to and accepted by all mankind. In a world which God "created according to His will," man is the only creature with decision-making capacities and responsibilities. God's name is "magnified and sanctified" whenever men make justice and compassion the basis of their personal conduct. Men advance the Kingship of God when they join others in concerted action for the abolition of ignorance, poverty, and corruption within their own society, and for the abolition of war as a means of resolving disputes between nations.

The study of Torah is the exalted means by which Israel "magnifies and sanctifies" the name of God in the world. Torah study aims to delineate the attitudes and deeds by which man sharpens the image of God, which is the sublime symbol of his human potential as a morally sensitive being.

Originally the *Kaddish* was recited after a session of Torah study, and great stress is laid in the Talmud on this response of the group to the *Kaddish* doxology: "May His great name be praised forever and unto eternity" (*Yehe shmeh rabba mevarakh le-alam ul-alme almaya)*. The earliest mention of this response is in Sifre, Deuteronomy 306, where Rabbi José refers to it. It is also mentioned several times in the Babylonian Talmud. Two references are particularly significant for an understanding of the meaning of the *Kaddish:* In the first, Rabbi José ben Ḥalafta (Palestine, second century) comments on the tragedy and pathos of Israel's exile from its homeland:

> Whenever Israel enters its houses of prayer and study and all join in the response *Yehe shmeh rabba,* the Holy One, blessed

be He, shakes His head and says, "Happy was the King when His children rendered Him such praise in His own abode. What made the Father send His own children into exile? Alas for the children who were exiled from their Father's table."

Talmud, Berakhot 3a

In the second passage, Rava (Babylonia, fourth century) contemplates the steadily worsening deterioration of morality and expresses the opinion that mankind is spared from being doomed by its misdeeds because as long as Israel sanctifies the name of God there is still hope for mankind's redemption.

> Each day is so much worse than the previous day that people are wont to say, "Would that tomorrow be not worse than yesterday." What then, saves the world from utter condemnation? The world is sustained by the *Kedushah de-Sidra** and by the response, *Yehe shmeh rabba,* uttered by the people at the conclusion of an Aggadic [homiletic] discourse.

Talmud, Sotah 49a

In both of these passages the *Kaddish* doxology is associated with a Torah discourse or with the study of Biblical texts. Still another passage depicts God as lauding Israel when it collectively utters another response of the *Kaddish;* and here too the context is one of Torah study:

> Rabbi Simeon taught: When is God exalted in this world? When His people Israel are gathered in their synagogues and

* We do not know when *Kedushah de-Sidra* was introduced into the synagogue service, but Rashi explains it as follows: *Kedushah de-Sidra* is a *Kedushah* service which was established at the end that all the people of Israel should engage in a minimum of Torah study every day. The Biblical portions are read with their Aramaic translation so that the untutored as well as the students can join in this. This combines two experiences: The sanctification of the Name [through the congregational recital of "Holy, holy, holy is the Lord of hosts, the whole earth is full of His glory" (Isaiah 6:3)] and the study of Torah. Therefore this is so dear [to God] (Talmud, Sotah 49a). In the daily morning service the *Kedushah de-Sidra* is identified with *Uva le-Tziyyon*. For a full analysis of *Uva le-Tziyyon,* see L. J. Liebreich, H. U. C. Annual, Vol. XXI, pp. 176-209.

> houses of study and when, after an *Aggadic* discourse by a sage, they respond: "Amen, may the name of the Lord be praised from now and unto eternity" [*Yehi shem Adonai mevorakh me-atah ve-ad olam*]. On hearing this, God rejoices that He is thus exalted in His world, and He says to His ministering angels, "Come and see how the people that I fashioned in My world, praise My name."
>
> *Midrash to Proverbs 14:28*

The full text of the *Kaddish* is first cited by Rabbi Amram Gaon (*ca.* 850 C.E.) in his classic work on the Prayer Book. Among the several versions of the *Kaddish* and the occasions when they are recited are the following:

Kaddish de-Rabbanan ("The Scholars' Kaddish")

This is recited after a Torah discourse or after a session of Torah study. It includes this appropriate prayer:

> Unto Israel and unto the scholars, unto their disciples and the disciples of their disciples, and unto all who pursue the study of Torah, here and everywhere, unto them and unto all of you may there be granted abundant peace, grace, lovingkindness, mercy, long life, ample sustenance, and deliverance by their Father, who is in heaven and on earth, and say ye, Amen.

Kaddish Shalem ("Complete Kaddish")

This is recited by the reader at the end of a congregational service. This *Kaddish* includes the following paragraph:

> May the prayers and petitions of all Israel be accepted before their Father, who is in heaven, and say ye, Amen.

Because the first word of the additional paragraph of the *Kaddish Shalem* is *Titkabbal,* it is also called *Kaddish Titkabbal*.

Ḥatzi Kaddish ("Half Kaddish")

This shortened form is recited by the reader at the end of each section of a congregational service.

***Kaddish Yatom* ("Mourner's Kaddish")**

The *Kaddish* doxology is recited by mourners after *Alenu* and after the recitation of one or more psalms. Scholars are of the opinion that originally a Torah session was conducted each day in the home of a mourner during the seven days of mourning ("Shivah"), and the mourner would recite the *Kaddish* after such a session. (It is still customary for the *Scholars' Kaddish* to be recited by mourners.) In time, the study session fell into disuse and the practice developed of mourners reciting the *Kaddish* after *Alenu* at the end of a service and at points during the service when psalms are recited, such as is the case in the Friday evening service after Psalms 92 and 93.

Though the *Mourner's Kaddish* has no reference to death, yet it is a highly appropriate means of honoring the memory of a departed dear one. It affirms the enduring significance of a human life, dedicated to the sanctification of the name of God, and implies a resolve on the part of the mourner to maintain Judaism as a way of life whereby the name of God is sanctified not only in words but also in deeds, which are "prayers in action."

The folk association of the recital of *Kaddish* by a mourner as the means of redeeming the soul of a departed parent has been traced to this legend about Rabbi Akiva: He met a man carrying a big load of wood on his shoulders. Akiva asked him why he was carrying the wood and the man told him that the wood was for the fire in Gehenna in which he was burned daily as punishment for having exploited the poor when he was a tax collector and that only when his son would recite *Barekhu* and *Kaddish* at a congregational service would his soul be redeemed from Gehenna. The legend continues to relate how Akiva located and educated the son to recite the *Kaddish* and *Barekhu* so that his father's soul be released from the fires of Gehenna (Tractate Kallah, ed. Higger, pp. 202-3).

Louis Ginzberg shows that the original version of this legend did not refer to *Kaddish* but to *Barekhu* and to the congregational response *Amen, yehe shmeh rabba* which in Geonic time was the customary congregational response to the recitation of *Barekhu* (Ginzberg, *Ginze Schechter,* Vol. I, pp. 235-236).

THE *MAARIV* (EVENING) SERVICE

Structure

The prescribed *Maariv* service, which follows the recital of the *Kabbalat Shabbat* psalms and hymns (which we have just examined), consists of five divisions:

I. *Barekhu:* The call to congregational worship;
II. The *Shema* and its blessings;
III. The *Amidah:* The central prayer, recited silently and in a standing position;
IV. The *Kiddush:* The "Sanctification of the Day" over the wine;
V. *Alenu:* The prayer for the universal acceptance of God's sovereignty.

The "core" of the *Maariv* service consists of items II and III, "The *Shema* and its blessings" and "The *Amidah.*"

Origins of the liturgy and unity among rites

What accounts for the essential *unity* of traditional Jewish worship the world over, despite a *diversity* characterized by over fifty variant liturgical rites? That which unites these rites is their conformance with stipulations laid down by the Rabbis regarding the content and structure of "The *Shema* and its blessings" and the prayers that comprise "The *Amidah.*"

The present fixed texts of the prayers originated in the ninth century C.E. when Rabbi Amram Gaon (*ca.* 850 C.E.), a Babylonian scholar, was asked to formulate rules governing the liturgy. He also gave the texts of the prayers. His aim was to eliminate from several prayers, circulating in certain quarters, passages which ran counter to Talmudic norms and to the basic teachings of Judaism.

Rabbi Amram Gaon's *Seder* became the basis of the various Sephardic rites. He was followed almost a century later by Saadiah Gaon (Egypt, *ca*. 925 C.E.) who issued his *Siddur* and added to the Hebrew text an Arabic translation of the prayers. In the twelfth century, Maimonides (1135-1204) issued his monumental legal code, *Mishneh Torah,* which includes, in the second of its fourteen parts, texts of the prayers and the liturgical rules to be followed. His text also won acceptance among the Sephardic communities of Spain, North Africa, Majorca, Sicily, and Egypt. In the main, the Sephardic rites followed the liturgical norms laid down by the Babylonian scholars. The Ashkenazic rites conformed to the decisions of the Palestinian scholars, and these rites are based on the work of Rabbi Simḥah ben Samuel of Vitry, France (*ca*. 1100 C.E.), author of *Maḥzor Vitry*. The Ashkenazic rites were adopted in Germany, Poland, Hungary, and Russia, and prevail in England, France, and North and South America.

There are discernible differences between the more than fifty rites of Jewish worship, especially in their selection of *Piyyutim* on festive occasions. But these differences have an overarching unity which is beautifully characterized by Professor Shalom Spiegel:

> The standard prayers, the oldest nucleus of the liturgy, always and everywhere became the center of Jewish worship, a bond of union despite geographical dispersal and a bridge across the ages linking the present with the past. At the same time, each period and place was left free, if not encouraged, to speak its own mind in new compositions added to or inserted within the ancient prayers . . . . Within the larger brotherhood of Israel and the stock of prayers common to all generations, the medieval synagogue attempts and maintains both a contemporary note and regional differences.*

The spiritual implication of a standard liturgy (see also pp. 149-151)

The word "liturgy" stems from the Greek *leitourgia* which is

* *The Jews, Their History, Culture and Religion,* ed. Louis Finkelstein, third ed. (New York: Harper and Row, 1960), p. 866.

a combination of *laos* (people) and *ergon* (work). Originally the word designated a function or office by which the individual rendered a service to the people. However, the Septuagint consistently translates the Hebrew word *Avodah* ("service") as *litourgas*. Hence the word came to denote a liturgical service of the people rather than *to* the people.

This particular meaning of the word accurately describes the spirit that animates Jewish prayer. It is essentially a service of praise and supplication by the people of Israel to affirm and confirm its collective dedication and obligation to God. This sense is conveyed in a prayer originally offered by the priests in the Temple imploring God to accept the daily sacrificial offerings of the people (Mishnah, Tamid 5:1). That prayer which is part of the three concluding *Berakhot* of each *Amidah* ("standing" or "silent prayer") reads as folows: "And may the service of Your people Israel be acceptable before You."

Collective awareness (see also pp. 149-151)

The collective awareness that pervades Jewish worship is characterized by Professor Abraham J. Heschel in these words:

> Judaism is not only the adherence to particular doctrines and observances, but primarily living in the Jews of the past and with the Jews of the present. Judaism is not only a certain quality in the souls of the individuals, but primarily the existence of the community of Israel . . . What we do as individuals is a trivial episode; what we attain as Israel causes us to become a part of Eternity.
>
> The Jew does not stand alone before God; it is as a member of the community that he stands before God. Our relationship to Him is not as an *I* to a *Thou,* but as a *We* to a *Thou.**

The *We* relationship to God is verbalized in the structured liturgy of Judaism. All of Jewish liturgy is suffused by the conviction that Israel is a founded people, divinely designated to serve on earth as living witnesses of God. Abraham is singled out in the Torah, to teach his descendants what God expects of man:

---

* A. J. Heschel, *Man's Quest for God* (New York: Charles Scribner's Sons, 1954), p. 45.

> For I have singled him out, that he may instruct his children and his posterity to keep the way of the Lord by doing what is right and just . . . (Genesis 18:19)

In the account of the Giving of the Torah, the entire people is told to prepare for its divinely ordained role among the peoples of mankind. When, after the Exodus, Moses is told to instruct the entire people to prepare for the revelation at Mount Sinai, he is to say to them:

> You have seen what I did to the Egyptians, how I bore you on eagles' wings and brought you to Me. Now then, if you will obey Me faithfully and keep My covenant, you shall be My treasured possession among all the peoples. Indeed, all the earth [*i.e.*, all humanity] is Mine, but you shall be to Me a kingdom of priests and a holy nation. (Exodus 19:4-6)

Remembering the Exodus (see also pp. 152-153)

The Torah (and indeed all of Scripture) reflects Israel's self-revelation to God, even as it mirrors those experiences in which God revealed Himself to the people. Scripture gives us, therefore, an intimate glimpse into that which transformed a horde of slaves into a people of great moral passion. The opening words, "You have seen what I did to the Egyptians," are fraught with powerful meaning which can be understood only in the light of a conception which is writ large in Biblical lore and law: *God freed His people from bondage and, as their Redeemer, made them His subjects by giving them commandments and a way of life which would be the mark of their new status as a people with whom He has established an indissoluble covenant.* They become His people even as He becomes their God, and in fact their new Master. Throughout Scripture, we hear reiterated, almost as a refrain, that the Exodus liberated this people from servitude so that they might become the servants of God.

In the eleventh century, Yehudah Halevi pointed out that the Ten Commandments do not open with the statement, "I, the Lord, am your God who created heaven and earth," but rather with the declaration, "I, the Lord, am your God who brought you out of the land of Egypt, the house of bondage" (Exodus 20:2). The implication is that as their Redeemer from bondage, God earned the prerogative of giving them commandments and demanding their exclusive worship of Him.* This idea is more explicitly expressed in the Book of Leviticus (25:55) which explains that in the jubilee year, hired or bound laborers must be set free together with their families: "For it is to Me that the Israelites are servants; they are My servants whom I freed from the land of Egypt."

Because the Exodus experience established God's claim on Israel, and their responsibility to adhere to God's will, the father of each family is instructed to tell his son the story of the Exodus—so that his posterity may regard it as a personal experience and thus feel obligated to obey God and keep His commandments.

> You shall say to your son, "We were slaves to Pharaoh in Egypt and the Lord freed us from Egypt with a mighty hand. . . . *Then the Lord commanded us to observe all these laws*. . . for our lasting good and for our survival . . ." (Deuteronomy 6:21-25)

The same relationship is stressed in the legal and holiness codes of the Pentateuch where the recurrent claim for obedience to God is that He liberated the people from slavery.**

The psalmist conveys the same thought when he states:

> And He *brought forth* His people with joy,
> His chosen ones with singing;
> And He gave them the lands of the nations,
> And they took the labors [wealth] of the
> peoples in possession;
> That they might keep His statutes
> And observe His laws. (Psalms 105:43-45)

The Rabbis based their rationale for the observance of the *Mitzvot* on the same thesis. Rabbi Yoḥanan ben Zakkai gives this allegorical explanation for the Biblical law (Exodus 21:6) which

---

* *Kuzari* 1, 25. Yehudah Halevi proceeds to say that Israel *was not* witness to the Creation, but *was* witness "to what I did to the Egyptians, etc." (Exodus 19:4).

** Exodus 29:46; Leviticus 22:33, 25:42, 25:55, 26:13, 26:45; Numbers 15:47; Deuteronomy 5:6, 13:6.

prescribes that when a slave refuses to accept his freedom his ear must be pierced:

> Why is it that of all the organs the ear alone is to be pierced? Rabbi Yoḥanan ben Zakkai interpreted this allegorically: God said, "It was the ear which heard Me say at Mount Sinai, 'The Israelites are My servants'; yet this man went and procured for himself another master—so let his *ear* be pierced."
>
> *Talmud, Kiddushin 22b*

The social legislation of the Torah is often linked to the redemption from Egyptian bondage. The laws protecting the rights of the stranger, the fatherless, and the widow are anchored in the recollection of the Exodus.

> You shall not subvert the rights of the stranger or the fatherless; you shall not take the widow's garment in pawn. Remember that you were a slave in Egypt and that the Lord your God redeemed you from there; therefore do I enjoin you to observe this commandment. (Deuteronomy 24:17-18)

Many ritual observances are associated with the recollection of the Exodus. Among them are the Passover festival (Exodus 12:17, Deuteronomy 16:1), the festival of Sukkot (Leviticus 23:43), the redemption of the first-born (Exodus 13:11-14), the rite of *Tefillin* (Exodus 13:16), and the offering of the first fruits (Deuteronomy 26:1-11).

"Remembrance of Creation" linked to "Remembrance of Exodus"

Finally, in the Deuteronomy version of the Ten Commandments, the observance of the Sabbath (described in the Exodus version as a "Remembrance of Creation") is associated with the Exodus:

> Remember the Sabbath day and keep it holy as the Lord your God has commanded you. . . . Remember that you were a slave in the land of Egypt and the Lord your God freed you from there with a mighty hand and an outstretched arm; therefore the Lord your God has commanded you to observe the Sabbath day. (Deuteronomy 5:12-15)

MAARIV: SABBATH EVENING SERVICE

Barekhu בָּרְכוּ

"Praise the Lord to whom praise is due"

In the Mishnah, the public recitation of the *Shema* and the blessings that accompany it is first on the list of liturgical occasions at which the presence of a *Minyan* is required (Mishnah, Megillah 4:3). It can therefore be assumed that the blessings were originally recited only at a congregational service. Later it became mandatory for a person to recite these blessings even where no *Minyan* was present.

Being part of a *Minyan* is in itself a religious experience. It is an event which affords the worshipers an opportunity to participate in an act of *Kiddush ha-Shem* ("Sanctification of the Name"). The *Barekhu* therefore expresses gratitude for the privilege of praying with a congregation *(Tzibbur)*.*

The reader invites the congregation: "Praise the Lord to whom praise is due" and the congregation responds, "Praised be the Lord, to whom praise is due, for ever and ever." The Palestinian Talmud (Berakhot 11b-c) discusses the seeming disregard here of the rule that in prayer one must always associate himself with the community. A twofold answer is offered. In the first place, the word *ha-Mevorakh* can be taken to mean "Who is praised by all," hence the reader is not really excluding himself from the *Klal* (community). In the second place, the reader must join the congregation in the response: "Praised be the Lord, to whom praise is due, for ever and ever." The word *Barukh* is connected with the Hebrew root *Barekh* ("to kneel"). This root occurs in, "Let us kneel before the Lord our Maker" (Psalms 95:6)

---

* Max Kadushin, *Worship and Ethics* (Northwestern University, 1964), p. 137.

and in, "He knelt down upon his knees" (II Chronicles 6:13). This association accounts for the direction given in the eleventh-century code *Orḥot Ḥayyim,* that one should bend forward when saying *Barukh* and resume the erect posture on the mention of the Name.

The two blessings before the evening *Shema*

The Mishnah (Berakhot 1:4) prescribes that in the evening the reading of the *Shema* is to be preceded by two blessings and followed by two blessings.*

The first blessing before the evening *Shema, Asher bi-d'varo maariv aravim* ("Who by His command brings on the evening twilight"), is a recognition that in the ordinary and regular orderliness of nature there is manifested the continuous activity of the ever-loving God.

The second blessing, *Ahavat Olam* ("With everlasting love"), is an expression of gratitude for the love which God bestowed upon Israel by making them the recipients of the Torah.

אֲשֶׁר בִּדְבָרוֹ מַעֲרִיב עֲרָבִים
Asher bi-d'varo maariv aravim
"Who by His command brings on the evening twilight"

This is the first blessing before the *Shema*. Here we express gratitude for the goodness of God as it is revealed to us in the calculable and dependable regularity of nature's laws. At dusk, day yields to night, and night is followed by the dawn of a new day. There are no capricious demons that man must cajole by magic and incantation. God's will is revealed in the harmony, design, and regularity of nature. Man is unique amidst the vastness of the universe, among the multitudinous variety of creatures that populate the earth. Though he is part of nature, he alone has the

---

* For the morning, the Mishnah prescribes two blessings before the *Shema* and one blessing after it. The total of seven blessings for the *Shema* of the morning and the evening inspired Rabbi Joshua ben Levi to invoke the verse from the Psalms (119:164): "Seven times a day do I praise Thee because of Thy righteous ordinances" (Palestinian Talmud, Berakhot 3c).

capacity to transcend "iron necessity." Though he is subject to unpredictable circumstance, he can creatively and courageously respond to what happens rather than merely react to it. He can turn an obstacle into a stepping stone to a higher self and deepen even in adversity his sensitivity and his dedication to those values which endow life with enduring significance.

"Creator of day and night."

Both day and night are mentioned to conform with the Rabbinic requirement that on mornings and evenings, the first blessing should refer to God as Creator of both light and darkness. The verse, "I form the light and create the darkness; I make peace and create evil" (Isaiah 45:7), is cited as the Scriptural reason for this requirement (Talmud, Berakhot 11b).

Scholars have suggested that the original intent may have been to negate and deny Zoroastrian and Gnostic dualisms which posited the existence of two primal powers, one that created light, the source of all that is good in the universe, and the other that created darkness, the source of all that is evil. Judaism resisted every nuance of dualism *(Shte Reshuyot)*. The Bible depicts Satan, the accuser of man in the celestial assizes, as being wholly subservient to the authority of God. In the first chapter of the Book of Job, Satan is portrayed as a malevolent influence who must however receive the approval of God when he proceeds to test the constancy of Job's integrity. The Rabbis were so meticulous in avoiding every taint of dualism, that they forbade the utterance of a prayer which said that God's name is "to be remembered and praised for all that is good," lest a conclusion be drawn that God is not to be remembered and praised even for the troubles that beset human life (Mishnah, Berakhot 5:3). The Mishnah rules that a person is obligated to praise God when trouble comes, just as he is obligated to praise Him when good fortune comes (*ibid.* 9:5). The Rabbis went as far as to forbid two consecutive recitations of the *Shema Yisrael* verse, lest such repetition be taken as the avowal of the existence of "two powers" (Talmud, Berakhot 33b).

"May our living and eternal God rule over us."

"God is near unto all who call upon Him" (Psalms 145:18).

He enters our life only when we invite Him and when we remain open and receptive to His luminous presence. This is the thrust of the conclusion of the first blessing before the *Shema*.

Ahavat Olam אַהֲבַת עוֹלָם
"With everlasting love"

In this, the second blessing that precedes the *Shema,* we thank God for the illumination of the Torah even as we express our gratitude in the first blessing for the physical light of the sun, the moon, and the stars. As in the first blessing, we do not look upon the Torah as a gift received by our forebears in ancient times and just handed down to us. The giving of the Torah is more than a historic reminiscence. It is a living experience. Every time we study the Torah we have a *Mattan Torah* experience. Through the study of Torah, God's love for Israel is freshly renewed. Thus we conclude this blessing, "Blessed art Thou . . . who *loves* His people Israel."

"For they [the teachings of Torah] are our life and the length of our days."

The study of Torah is deemed the indispensable means of Israel's existence as a people. This is magnificently reflected in the following Rabbinic tale:

> Once the wicked government [Rome] decreed that Jews must no longer occupy themselves with the study and teaching of Torah. One day, Pappus ben Judah (*ca.* 135 C.E.) found Rabbi Akiva gathering assemblies and teaching Torah. "Are you not afraid of the wicked government?" he asked Rabbi Akiva. In reply, Rabbi Akiva told Pappus the parable of the fox who from the bank of the stream saw some schools of fishes swimming rapidly from one place to another. When the fox asked them from what they were fleeing, they said that they were fleeing from the nets which men had spread against them. The fox then invited them to come up on dry land and dwell together with him in peace and harmony. "You are not the shrewdest of animals," the fish said to the fox, "you are a

fool. If we are in danger in the water which is our life-element, how much more would we be endangered in a place which is our death-element'' (Talmud, Berakhot 61b).

''We will meditate on them day and night.''

The Palestinian Talmud characterizes *Ahavat Olam* as *Birkat ha-Torah,* (''the blessing over the Torah''). It is a *Mitzvah* to devote some time every day and every night to the study of Torah. The ''reading'' of the *Shema,* which consists of three selections from the Torah, is therefore an occasion for thanking God for the *Mitzvah* that is in fulfillment of the verse, ''This book of the Torah shall not depart out of your mouth but you shall meditate on it day and night''* (Joshua 1:8).

Israel is the beloved people of God not by superiority of numbers, power, or dominion. Whenever the liturgy speaks of Israel as God's most favored nation it unfailingly refers to the giving of the Torah. The Torah gives us a heightened consciousness of our common spiritual origin and of our shared commitment to the task of translating its luminous ideals into life.

The belief that the entire people of Israel was the recipient of the Torah served to make Judaism hospitable to a broad expansion of the concept of Torah and saved it from a rigid, ossified biblicism. The Oral Law came to be regarded as the living and authentic interpretation of the Written Law. Rabbi Ḥaggai even asserted that the Oral Law takes precedence over the Written Law, and another scholar said that on Mount Sinai there were revealed to Moses all the teachings of future scholars (Palestinian Talmud, Pe-ah 17a). In actual usage, the word Torah was invested with a wider meaning than that of a particular book or a series of books. It came to denote a continual process of study and interpretation by means of which the teachings of the Torah continued to be a Torah of life to succeeding generations. This process was described by Rabbi Kook as one by means of which ''the old is renewed and the new is made sacred.''

While it would be a gross exaggeration to attribute to the

* The actual meaning of *ve-Hagita Bo* in this verse and elsewhere where *Hagah* occurs is not ''you shall meditate on it'' but rather ''you shall speak of it,'' and this accounts for the phrase ''out of your mouth.''

Rabbis and their successors through the centuries a concept of progressive development, it is nevertheless striking how they came to regard Torah as a growing, cumulative process of dialectics, interpretation, and reinterpretation by means of which Judaism was redeemed from an undiscerning sacralization of the past. The written word was regarded as flexible and replete with surprising insights. This is the implication of Ben Bag-Bag's dictum: "Turn it [the Torah] this way and turn it that way, for everything is in it" (Mishnah, Avot 5:22). An even bolder extension of the concept of Torah is conveyed in the Rabbinic statement that when two scholars offer mutually contradictory opinions both can be regarded as "The words of the living God" (Talmud, Eruvin 13b). To continue to be a viable religion, a perennial Tree of Life, the Torah must be regarded as a ceaseless process of revelation for the voice heard at Sinai never ceased (Onkelos on Deuteronomy 5:19).

THE *SHEMA*

The "Kingship of God" and the "yoke of the Mitzvot"

> Rabbi Judah said in the name of Rav: When one is out walking and the time for reading the *Shema* has arrived, one must stop and stand and accept the yoke of the Kingship of God. How does one accept the Kingship of God? [By reciting] *Shema Yisrael* (Deuteronomy Rabbah 2:31).

> Rabbi Joshua ben Korḥa said: Why do we read *Shema-Ve-ahavta* before *Vehayah Im Shamoa?* Because one must first accept the yoke of the Kingship of Heaven before accepting the yoke of the *Mitzvot* (Mishnah, Berakhot 2:2).

> A king of flesh and blood, upon entering a province, was advised by his attendants to issue decrees to the populace. He refused to do so and said, "If they will not first accept my kingship they will not accept my decrees." Likewise, God said to Israel, "I, the Lord, am your God who brought you out of the land of Egypt, the house of bondage," [and then He said,] "You shall have no other gods besides Me" (Mekhilta, ed. Horowitz-Rabin, p. 222).

The above cited passages indicate that two basic Rabbinic concepts are associated with the *Shema:* "The yoke of the Kingship of Heaven" and "The yoke of the *Mitzvot.*"

Accepting the "yoke of the Kingship of God"

We have seen above that Heaven *(Shamayim)* was used as a metonym for God in order not to pronounce the Tetragrammaton (Adonai) when not engaged in prayer or in the study of Scripture. "The Kingship of Heaven" means therefore, "The Kingship of God."

For some centuries prior to the Mishnaic period, Jewish sectarian circles gave the concept, "Kingship of Heaven," an other-worldly emphasis. They made it a symbol not of the redemption *of* the world, but rather of man's redemption *from* the world. This emphasis may have been due to a popular disillusionment with the rule of the descendants of the Maccabeans whose forebears had freed Palestine from the Syrian-Greeks (168-65 B.C.E.). The Hasmonean rulers, descendants of the Maccabees, had become subservient to the Romans who occupied Palestine in 63 B.C.E., with Pompey's entry into Jerusalem. The corrupt practices of the Hasmonean high priests and kings and the cruel treatment of the people by the Roman procurators induced apocalyptic visions of an imminent end of the world and of the coming of a Messianic era, when the Roman "government of arrogance" *(Malkhut Zadon)* would be crushed, and when the righteous would be redeemed and then translated to a celestial "Kingdom of God."

Sects nurtured by despair and bred by disillusionment practiced celibacy and strict asceticism. They recoiled from communal concerns and some even lived in caves, such as the Qumran caves where the Dead Sea Scrolls were discovered in 1947. Others, such as the Judeo-Christian sect, remained in the cities but did not join those who actively resisted the Romans. They believed that the end of the world was imminent and that the Messiah would come to redeem them from their foreign oppressors. These sects were under the influence of apocalyptic books only one of which, the Book of Daniel, won admittance into the canon of the Hebrew Scriptures. The other apocalyptic books were preserved in a Greek translation and are included in the Apocrypha and the Pseudo-Epigrapha. The Rabbis classified them as external books, banned from public reading at a synagogue service (Talmud, Shabbat 116b).

Aware of the tendency to denigrate and derogate life on earth by the riveting of attention on a hoped-for transformation to a "Kingdom of Heaven," the Rabbis discouraged such escapist views. True, they had a firm belief in the resurrection of the body and said that one who rejects this belief would have no share in the world to come (Mishnah, Sanhedrin 10:1). They had an equally strong belief in the coming of the Messiah. But their major emphasis was on the urgency of performing one's duty conscientiously in life here on earth.

For the Rabbis, the "Kingdom of God" was not one to be established at a future time beyond history. Literally the word *Malkhut* means not "kingdom" but "kingship." The "Kingdom of God" is already here. God is King of the universe since He established the laws of heaven and earth (Jeremiah 33:25). It is not the *Kingdom* of God that needs to be established but rather the *Kingship* of God by which is meant, the acceptance by men of the sovereignty of God in their lives. Since man is a morally free, autonomous being, he is expected to "accept upon himself" the yoke of the Kingship of God.

We have said above that the sovereignty of God is a this-worldly rather than an other-worldly concept. Despite the bitter plight of Jewry in the two centuries before the Common Era, the accent was not placed on a celestial Kingdom of God, but on the extension of the Kingship of God on earth. Thus, Rabbi Akiva, who died as a martyr during the Hadrianic persecutions (135 C.E.), sponsored Bar Kokhba and hailed him as the Messiah, while other colleagues considered him an impostor (Palestinian Talmud, Taanit 68d). Rabbi Yoḥanan ben Zakkai, who witnessed the destruction of the second Temple, founded the Academy of Yavneh where surviving scholars and their disciples continued to pursue their studies. Because he was a man of vision and action, he formulated in words of penetrating significance the advice that he gave his disciples shortly before his death, the teaching that faith in a Messianic redemption must not diminish one's ardor for the task that calls for action now, for fantasy must not make us blind to fact.

> If while you are holding a sapling in your hand, they come and say to you, "The Messiah has arrived," first plant the sapling and then go to greet the Messiah (Avot de-Rabbi Nathan 2, chap. 31).

The Kingship of God is not a remote celestial ideal; it needs to be realized in our personal lives and communal lives by the uncoerced volition of men who exercise their congenital power to "choose the good and reject the evil."

Accepting the "yoke of the Mitzvot"

Judaism is more than a creed, a belief, an identity, or an affiliation. It is a way of living in which the individual Jew concretizes the moral and spiritual values which comprise the ideals it fosters. Judaism is given form and content when one "accepts on himself the yoke of the *Mitzvot*." In Rabbinic times, the imaginative concept was stressed, and it was taught that the soul of every Jew was present at Sinai. Every Jew is therefore "under a binding oath" since Mount Sinai to observe the *Mitzvot* (Talmud, Yoma 73b).

While the attitude that we are sworn to the *Mitzvot* since Sinai is most suggestive and inspiring, it runs counter to our contemporary temper to accentuate its coercive overtones. We live in a free society which welcomes and even encourages a pluralism of religious belief and practice. Jews who feel and practice a total commitment to the faith of their fathers and its observances need to learn that, just as their own religious freedom rests on religious diversity, the times in which we live call for the acceptance of religious pluralism within Judaism. It is neither desirable nor feasible in a free society for Judaism to be an authoritarian, homogenized, and monolithic regimen of religious conformance. Because temperaments and environmental conditions differ, we must expect and accept a wide variety of religious observance. Indeed, the meticulous pietist must learn to accept and respect a fellow Jew who is less meticulous in his observance and who does not respond to all the demands of the tradition. The liberal Jew, whose observance of *Mitzvot* is much more selective, must learn to respect the deeper commitment of those who are not as permissive as he. We must learn to influence one another and to enhance one another's life not by exhortation but by example, and not by coercion but by persuasion. Our love for Judaism must never exceed our love for Jews, for in such an imbalance we tend to forget the lesson taught in this pertinent passage:

> I was asked by a certain man, "I have in my heart two great loves: the Torah and the people of Israel. But I do not know which takes precedence over the other." I answered him, "People are wont to say that the Torah comes first, for Scripture says, 'The Lord made me as the beginning of His ways' (Proverbs 8:22), but I would say that the sacred people of Israel comes first for Scripture says, 'Israel is sacred to the Lord, His first fruits of the produce' (Jeremiah 2:3)."
>
> *Seder Eliyahu Rabbah, p. 71*

We can distill from the terms "Accepting the yoke of the *Kingship of God*" and "Accepting the yoke of the *Mitzvot*" two supremely important principles to guide us in our desire to live as Jews in a free and open society. These terms can serve to warn us against the idolatries men follow in their zeal for the present as they reject their commitment to "Our God and God of our fathers." These idolatries result from the absolutization of lesser loyalties that are a denial and repudiation of God. Some absolutize sensualism and call it self-realization. They deify lust and call it love. They defy self-control and self-discipline in the name of self-fulfillment. They abolish self-respect in the name of self-liberation. Theirs is the mistaken notion that all that is new is true and all that is old is obsolete. Judah L. Magnes warned us against such idolatrous loyalties in these incisive words:

> It is the Jew's historical function to question, to challenge, to deny every idolatry which the world in its self-delusion comes to worship, whether this idolatry be of nature, science or of

state and society—and beyond these, to point to God. This is his real reason for existence.*

The expression "yoke of the commandments [*Mitzvot*]" can serve to remind us of the Rabbinic principle: "Greater is he who is commanded and observes than he who is not commanded and observes" (Talmud, Kiddushin 31a). To apply this to our contemporary situation we can paraphrase this as follows: "Greater is he whose observance of the *Mitzvot* is prompted by an inner feeling of obligation than he who observes the *Mitzvot* without an inner feeling of obligation."

Unless we resolve to live as "commanded Jews," our pattern of religious life will be casual, optional, sporadic, and devoid of the sense of *Mitzvah* which is the concept by which Judaism is distinct and distinguished among the religions of mankind.

On pronouncing the *Shema*

The Mishnah rules that the *Shema* be spoken with the meticulous pronunciation of every syllable in each word (Berakhot 2:3). Both in the Palestinian and in the Babylonian Talmud, one is cautioned against the conflation of certain words and syllables, and against the mispronunciation of certain words (Palestinian Talmud, Berakhot 4d; Babylonian Talmud, Berakhot 15b). One of these cautions relates to the correct pronunciation of the *Zayyin* in *Lemaan Tizkeru* ("that you may remember"). With the articulate pronunciation of the *Zayyin,* the verse means: "That you may remember to observe all My commandments . . ." But with the *Zayyin* mispronounced as an "s," the verse would seem to say: "In order that you may be rewarded *(Tiskeru)* for observing all My commandments" (Palestinian Talmud, Berakhot 4d).

The order of the three sections

The three sections of the *Shema* are not recited in the order in which they occur in the Torah, the third section, from the Book of Numbers, being recited after the two sections from the Book of

* Quoted in *Argument and Doctrine,* ed. Arthur A. Cohen (Harper & Row, 1970), p. 278.

Deuteronomy. Two explanations are offered. Rabbi Joshua ben Korḥa said:

> Why do we read *Shema-Ve-ahavta* before *Vehayah Im Shamoa?* Because one must first accept the yoke of the Kingship of Heaven before accepting the yoke of the *Mitzvot* (see pp. 83-88). Why does *Vehayah Im Shamoa* precede *Vayomer?* Because the latter makes reference to the *Tzitzit,* a *Mitzvah* which is to be observed only during the day, while in *Vehayah* we are told "And you shall teach them to your children," and the *Mitzvah* of studying and teaching the Torah devolves on us both day and night (Mishnah, Berakhot 2:2).

Rabbi Simeon ben Yoḥai suggests this additional reason:

> The sections are arranged in the descending order of their comprehensiveness. The first section is most important because it stresses the threefold duty to learn, to teach, and to practice. The second accentuates the twofold duty to learn and to practice, while the third underscores only the duty to practice (Talmud, Berakhot 14b).

COMMENTS ON THE TEXT

El melekh ne-eman–"God, the faithful King"

When the *Shema* is read in private devotion, the words: *El Melekh Ne-eman* ("God, the faithful King"), forming the acrostic *Amen,* are read before the *Shema.* When one recites the *Shema* at a congregational service, these three words are omitted. Instead, the reader concludes the *Shema* with the words: *Adonai Elohekhem Emet* ("the Lord your God is faithful"). The reason offered is that there are 245 words in the text of the *Shema,* and by adding three words the total becomes 248, symbolizing the 248 parts of the human body and thus indicating that one should love God with every fibre of his being (Tur Oraḥ Ḥayyim, 61).

Another reason for saying *El Melekh Ne-eman* in private

worship only is based on Rabbi Ḥanina's interpretation (Talmud, Shabbat 119b) that "*Amen* is an abbreviation of the three words *El Melekh Ne-eman.*" Since it is deemed improper for a person to respond *Amen* to a liturgical blessing which he himself recites,* the words *El Melekh Ne-eman* are said instead. At a congregational service, however, these three words are omitted, since the individual can recite *Amen* upon hearing the Reader conclude the two required blessings before the *Shema* with the words, "Who loves His people Israel."

Shema Yisrael שְׁמַע יִשְׂרָאֵל

"Hear, O Israel" (Deuteronomy 6:4)

"Hear, O Israel, the Lord [is] our God, the Lord [is] One." (6:4)

In the new Torah translation of the Jewish Publication Society, the last phrase is rendered, "the Lord alone" and this is the meaning given by Ibn Ezra and Rashbam in their commentaries. The association of *Eḥad* with the philosophical concept of monotheism was due to the desire of Maimonides and other Jewish philosophers to negate the trinitarian claims of Christianity. Max Kadushin calls our attention to the fact that there were other forms of monotheism, such as pantheism and stoicism, which Judaism also rejected.**

***Eḥad* ("One")**

The pronunciation of the word *Eḥad* is prolonged so that the

* The only exception is in the *Birkat ha-Mazon* where the third blessing concludes with the words, "Who in mercy will rebuild Jerusalem. Amen" (Talmud, Berakhot 45b). The exception is made because *Amen* serves here to set apart the three Biblically prescribed blessings of the *Birkat ha-Mazon* that have just been concluded, from the fourth blessing, *ha-Tov ve-ha-Metiv* ("Who brings good and will bring good") which, as a Rabbinical enactment *(de-Rabbanan),* is of secondary importance compared to the first three blessings, which have the weight of Biblical authority behind them *(de-Oraita)* (Talmud, Berakhot 46a, 48b).

** Max Kadushin, *Worship and Ethics* (Northwestern University, 1964), pp. 184-185.

individual might mentally affirm God's exclusive sovereignty, "above and below and in all four directions" (Talmud, Berakhot 13b; cf. Rashi *ad locum*).

In the scroll of the Torah, the *"Ayyin"* of *Shema* and the *"Dalet"* of *Eḥad* are written in enlarged form. These form the word *Ed* ("witness") and this is said by Abudarham (*ca.* fourteenth century) to be taken as a reminder that a Jew must live as a witness to God's Kingship.

Barukh shem kevod malkhuto le-olam va-ed

"Blessed be the name of His glorious Kingship for ever and ever."

In the Temple the response to the mention of God's name in praise of Him was not *"Amen"* but *"Barukh shem kevod malkhuto leolam va-ed."* The recitation of *Barukh Shem* immediately after the *Shema* underscores the liturgical meaning of the *Shema* as the acceptance of the Kingship of God (see pp. 84-86). According to Rabbi Abbahu, the Palestinian Jews adopted the practice of reciting *Barukh Shem* aloud, though it interrupts the continuity of Biblical verses of the *Shema,* lest the Judeo-Christians claim that some qualification of the absolute unity of God was then being recited. In Babylonia, where there were no Christians, *Barukh Shem* was recited in an undertone, since it is an interpolation into the *Shema* which is a Biblical text (Talmud, Pesaḥim 56a).

In his biography of Akiba, Louis Finkelstein advances an intriguing historical explanation of its silent recitation. During the Hadrianic persecutions (125-135 C.E.) the public recitation of the *Shema* was prohibited, probably because it implied a denial of the divinity of the Roman emperor. To circumvent this interdiction, the Jews would recite the *Shema* under their breath so that the Roman soldiers who stood guard at the door might not overhear them (Tosefta, Berakhot 2:13). The response *Barukh Shem* was especially objectionable to the Romans since it directly referred to God's Kingship, and hence it was whispered. But on Yom Kippur, the Jews, even in the days of fierce persecution, would not suppress the affirmation of their faith, and they shouted the interdicted words no matter how dangerous that might be. The silent response of *Barukh Shem,* was retained even after the persecutions were lifted.*

For the Midrashic explanation of the exception made on Yom Kippur, see p. 96.

Ve-ahavta וְאָהַבְתָּ

"You shall love the Lord" (Deuteronomy 6:5-9)

"You shall love the Lord your God with all your heart, with all your soul, and with all your might." (6:5)

The first section (Deuteronomy 6:4-9) affirms that God alone is to be our God. When we say that God is One, we declare that all our loyalties are conditioned by the primary loyalty owed to Him alone. We are to love God with all that we have and with all that we are. If love, any love, is to be more than a casual experience, it must be founded on the consciousness of the proximity of the beloved. The love of God is articulated in the nearness of God, in the fact that it will inspire diligent efforts to teach "these words" to our children, to make these teachings the guideposts of our daily life, evening and morning, when at home and when abroad. As reminders of this supreme loyalty, "these words" are to be placed on the arm and on the forehead *(Tefillin)* and inscribed on the doorposts *(Mezuzah)*.

"Impress them upon your children" (6:7)

The Grace After Meals *(Birkat ha-Mazon),* includes a supplication that the Merciful One bless, "my father, my teacher, and my mother, my teacher." The primary responsibility for character training rests with parents, and a school system fails when parents become dropout teachers. In the religious school the child can be taught to know Judaism by studying it, but in the home he can be taught to love Judaism by living it.

---

* Louis Finkelstein, *Akiba* (Convici Friede, New York, 1936), p. 252.

"Bind them as a sign on your hand." (6:8)

Within man there is a constant tension between his animality and his humanity. He needs to govern and transcend the urges of his animality in order to educate those rational and emotional aspirations which express his humanity. Sacred symbols such as the *Tefillin* and the *Mezuzah* are not magical in purpose. They are to serve as permanent reminders of the link between man and God.

Vehayah im shamoa וְהָיָה אִם־שָׁמֹעַ

"If you obey My commandments" (Deuteronomy 11:13-21)

The second section of the *Shema* is also taken from the Book of Deuteronomy. In the context in which it is found, Moses tells the people that unlike the soil of Egypt which was cultivated largely by irrigation, the land of Canaan which they were about to occupy depended on rain—which is a gift of God. Because it is "a land on which the Lord your God always keeps His eye from year's beginning to year's end" (Deuteronomy 11:12), the people are warned that the indispensable rainfall would be withheld if they allowed themselves to be lured into the worship of strange gods (*ibid.* 11:17). Indeed, the prophet Hosea chastises his contemporaries for straying from the worship of the imageless God of Israel and adopting the pagan worship of Baal, who was believed to be the dispenser of rain and fertility: "She did not know that it was I that gave her the corn, the wine, and the oil, and multiplied unto her silver and gold which they used for Baal" (Hosea 2:10). As further punishment for the violation of their covenant with God, they would be driven into exile from the very land which God had given them. As frequent reminders of the promise and the warning, "these words" are to be inserted in the capsules of the *Tefillin* and inscribed on the parchment of the *Mezuzah*. However unsophisticated the second paragraph of the *Shema* may be, it offers a concrete warning that the moral law cannot be violated with impunity.

Modern history has confirmed all too accurately that in the wake of idolatries based on racial and class imperialisms, severe economic hardship and tragic dislocations of peoples result. The interdependence of moral integrity and physical security can be seen to have a global significance, for the effects of the maltreatment of the weak by the strong offer horrifying validation of the warning here expressed with such simple profundity.

Vayomer וַיֹּאמֶר

"The Lord said to Moses: Speak to the Israelites . . . to make fringes on the corners of their garments"
(Numbers 15:37-41)

In this, the third section of the *Shema,* mention is made of the fringes *(Tzitzit)* which the Israelites are to put on their garments, with a blue thread on the fringe of each corner. "Let them attach a cord of blue to the fringe at each corner" (Numbers 15:38). The use of the cord of blue was no longer in vogue in *Amoraic* times (*ca.* 300 C.E.), and the Talmud indicates that the *Ḥillazon* (murex), from the blood of which the blue coloring was extracted, virtually became extinct as it made its appearance once in seventy years (Menaḥot 44a). Another Talmudic tradition alludes to *Luz* as the town from which the blue thread was imported (Sanhedrin 12a). In referring to the fringes, the Torah focuses attention on the cord of blue when it says, "Look at it [*i.e.,* the cord of blue] and recall all the commandments of the Lord and observe them so that you do not follow your heart and eyes in your lustful urge" (Numbers 15:39).*

The exact symbolism of the blue cord is uncertain. We know from later books of the Bible that the color blue came to be regarded as a sign of regal splendor. This is evident in the description of Mordecai's appointment to the post formerly held by Haman: "Mordecai went forth from the king in royal apparel of blue and white" (Esther 8:15). In this connection it is germane to speak of the Mishnaic law which rules that "sons of kings" may go out on Sabbath from the home into the public domain with golden

---

* A full discussion of this fascinating subject is to be found in Ben Zion Bokser's article, "The Thread of Blue" in the *Proceedings of the American Academy for Jewish Research,* Vol. 31, 1962, pp. 1-32. On the Rabbinic interpretation of the cord of blue, see p. 101.

bells on the outer garment (Mishnah, Shabbat 6:9). This passage inspired Rabbi Simeon to make the observation that all Israelites may wear garments with golden bells because all Israelites are of royal ancestry (Talmud, Shabbat 67a).

SELECTED RABBINIC COMMENTS

"Hear, O Israel, the Lord [is] our God, the Lord [is] One." (Deuteronomy 6:4)

The ministering angels in the celestial regions are not permitted to invoke the name of God until Israel has first done so on earth by reciting the *Shema*. Scripture says, "When the morning stars sang together, and all the sons of God shouted for joy" (Job 38:7). The morning stars are Israel, for Israel is likened to the stars (Genesis 22:17). The sons of God are the ministering angels, as Scripture says: "The sons of God came to present themselves before the Lord" (Job 1:6).

Sifre, Deuteronomy 306; cf. Talmud, Ḥullin 91b

"Hear, O Israel!" (6:4)

When God looks down on the earth and sees how pagan theaters and circuses, centers of lust and violence, thrive securely and undisturbed while His own Temple is in ruins, He is so wrought up that He threatens to destroy the world. However, as soon as Israel enters its synagogues and schools and recites, "Hear, O Israel," God's wrath is appeased for the sake of Israel.

Yalkut, Va-etḥanan 836

"The Lord [is] our God, the Lord [is] One [alone]." (6:4)

When a human king sends his legions into battle, they refuse to fight when he fails to provide them with the food they require. Very different is our relationship with God. When He provides us with food, He alone is our God, but even when He subjects us to starvation, He alone is our God.

Yalkut, Va-etḥanan 835

"Blessed be the name of His glorious Kingship for ever and ever."

Originally *Barukh Shem* was recited by the angels. Moses brought this declaration of the angels down to Israel but he instructed them to say it silently. Why? In explanation Rabbi Assi told this parable: Once a man stole a jewel from the king's palace. When he gave it to his wife, he said to her, "Do not wear it publicly, wear it only in the house." For this reason *Barukh Shem* is always recited silently. Why then does Israel recite it aloud on Yom Kippur? Because the people of Israel are on Yom Kippur as pure as the angels, they can say aloud, "Blessed be the name of His glorious Kingship for ever and ever."

Deuteronomy Rabbah 2:36

"And you shall love the Lord your God." (6:5)

Elsewhere we are commanded to fear Him (Deuteronomy 10:20). When we approach a mortal ruler, we submit our request with trepidation, even with dread, and we feel much relieved when we leave his presence. Because we fear him we avoid too frequent contacts with him. Very different is our feeling about God. Our fear and awe of Him are suffused with the love one feels for an intimate friend. Only between man and God can there be such harmonious blending of fear and love.

Sifre, Deuteronomy 32

"And you shall love the Lord your God." (6:5)

By a change in vocalization, the text can be so read to mean: You shall make others love God. How? You must be scrupulously honest in your business dealings, you must be fair in your conduct in the market place and in your relationships with all people. Then you will influence others to love God. When a man is scrupulously honest and consistently upright and that man also studies Bible and Mishnah, a person observing him will say, "So and So is fortunate, So and So studies Torah. Alas, my father did not teach me Torah. So and So did study Torah and look how noble are his deeds. By the Temple itself, I resolve to teach my children

Torah.'' Thus that man sanctifies the name of God by his conduct. But not so is the case of the man who is unscrupulous in his business dealings, whose behavior in the market place is corrupt, and whose dealings with his fellow men are devious. When such a man studies Bible and Mishnah, a person observing him will say: ''Woe to So and So who studies Torah! To be commended indeed was my father who did not teach me Torah. Look at So and So! He studied Torah and see how reprehensible are his actions. By the Temple itself, I resolve never to teach my children Torah.'' Thus that man has desecrated the name of God by his conduct.

Therefore, act so that all will love you, Jew and Gentile alike. For if one steals from a Gentile he will end up stealing from a Jew, and if one steals from a Jew, he will end up stealing from a Gentile. The Torah was given to Israel so that God's name may be sanctified, for Scripture says: ''And they shall declare My glory among the nations'' (Isaiah 66:19).

Seder Eliyahu Rabbah, p. 140; cf. Talmud, Yoma 86a

"With all your heart." (6:5)

''Here the word for heart is *levav* not *lev*. This suggests that we must love God with our two inclinations: with our evil inclination as well as with our good inclination.''

Mishnah, Berakhot 9:5

"With all your soul." (6:5)

When the Romans brought Rabbi Akiva out to be executed, they first combed his body with iron combs. As it was time for reading the *Shema,* he began its recitation, and despite the tortures to which he was being subjected, he continued to take upon himself the yoke of the Kingship of God. His disciples said to him, ''Master, are you so insensitive to pain?'' Rabbi Akiva answered them: ''All my life I have been troubled with this verse: 'You shall love your God . . . with all your soul . . .' This means: even if He takes your life. I have been thinking: When will I have the opportunity to fulfill this? Now that the opportunity is here, shall I not fulfill it?'' He prolonged the word *Eḥad* (One) and the word was on his lips as he expired. A heavenly voice then proclaimed, "Happy are you, Rabbi Akiva, that you died with *Eḥad* on your lips."

Talmud, Berakhot 61b

"With all your might." (6:5)

Meod (might) reminds us of the words *Middah* (measure) and *Modeh* (grateful). This suggests the teaching: "Whatever measure He metes out to you, be exceedingly [*Meod*] grateful to Him."

Mishnah, Berakhot 9:5

"With all your heart, with all your soul, and with all your might." (6:5)

Rabbi Eliezer asked, "After we are told that we should love God with all our life, what need is there to tell us to love Him with all our might [wealth]? There are people to whom possessions seem to be more more precious than life [for they shorten their life in pursuit of wealth]. Such people are bidden to love God with all their wealth."

Talmud, Berakhot 61b

"Impress them upon your children." (6:7)

Rabbi Ḥiyya ben Abba saw Rabbi Joshua ben Levi wearing festive clothes when he brought his grandchild to school. He asked, "Why this festive attire?" Rabbi Joshua replied, "Is this not an occasion of supreme importance? Bringing a grandchild to the study of the Torah is like experiencing again the giving of the Torah at Sinai." From that time on, Rabbi Ḥiyya would not eat his morning meal until he had taught his son a Torah lesson.

Talmud, Kiddushin 30a

Rabbi Joshua ben Levi said, "He who teaches Torah to his grandchild is considered as if he were personally receiving the Torah at Sinai. This we learn from the passage in the Torah, 'Make them known to your children and your children's children'

(Deuteronomy 4:9), which is followed by the verse, 'The day that you stood before the Lord your God at Horeb' (*ibid.* 4:10)."

Talmud, Kiddushin 30a

In another verse we are told, "Make them known to your children and your *children's children*" (Deuteronomy 4:9). This teaches us that he who educates his child in the knowledge of the Torah is considered as if he were giving Torah instruction to his children, his grandchildren, and indeed, to future generations for all time to come.

Talmud, Kiddushin 30a

Rabbi Judah said in the name of Rav, "Truly, Rabbi Joshua ben Gamla (*ca.* 64 B.C.E.) should be remembered for good, for had it not been for him, the Torah would have been forgotten in Israel." Formerly only a child who had a father was taught the Torah and the child who had no father was not taught . . . Then Rabbi Joshua ben Gamla ordered that teachers should be appointed in every district and in every town and that the children be enrolled at the ages of six or seven years."

Talmud, Bava Batra 21a

"If, then, you will obey the commandments that I enjoin upon you this day." (Deuteronomy 11:13)

You must not disregard My commandments as one disregards a king's obsolete decrees. You must always look upon them as decrees that were given to you *this* day—decrees which a person is eager to read and obey.

Sifre, Deuteronomy 33

"If, then, you will obey the commandments." (11:13)

The Hebrew reads: *Im shamoa tishmeu*. *Shamoa* means "to obey," *Tishmeu* means "to understand." This teaches us that by understanding what we have previously learned, we can absorb more knowledge.

Sifre, Deuteronomy 48

"This day." (11:13)

Say not, "I cannot master the entire Torah and observe all its *Mitzvot,*" because we are told that "The measure thereof is longer than the earth and broader than the sea" (Job 11:9). Such erroneous thinking is reflected in this parable: A king asked his son to hire two men to fill a deep pit. The first, a stupid worker, looked into the pit and exclaimed in despair, "How can I fill so deep a cavern?" The other, a wise worker, said, "What concern is it of mine that the pit is so deep? I am hired by the day and I shall therefore perform my day's work." So God says to us: "What concern is it of yours that the Torah is so extensive and that there is so much to learn? You are hired to do My work from day to day. All that I expect of you is to perform a full day's work in the study of Torah."

Yalkut, Ekev 863

"I will give grass in your field for your cattle, and you shall eat . . ." (11:15)

It is forbidden to partake of food before one has fed his animals. For the Torah mentions first the food for the cattle and this implies that only then you may eat.

Talmud, Berakhot 40a

"Thus you shall eat your fill . . . Take care not to . . . serve other gods." (11:15-16)

Moses said to them, "Beware, lest you rebel against God, for when a man is satiated and prosperous he tends to feel self-sufficient and to rebel against God . . ." An example of the corrosion of character that prosperity can bring is that of the people of Sodom. They said, "We are not dependent on others, for we have more than enough food and gold and silver. Let us pass a law forbidding the poor to enter our land."

Sifre, Deuteronomy 43

"Instruct them to make for themselves fringes."
(Numbers 15:38)

Why is this section included in the *Shema?* Because it speaks of five important themes: The *Mitzvah* of *Tzitzit,* our liberation from Egyptian bondage, the duty of observing the commandments, the warning to abstain from lust, and the admonition to abstain from idolatry. The first three are directly mentioned, while the last two are implied in the verse, "That ye go not after your own heart and your own eyes, after which ye used to go astray" (Numbers 15:39).

Talmud, Berakhot 12b

"Let them attach a cord of blue to the fringe at each corner." (15:38)

Rabbi Meir said: "Why was the color blue singled out from all other colors? Because blue resembles the sea and the sea resembles the sky and the sky resembles the Throne of Glory."

Talmud, Menaḥot 43b

"On the corners of their garments." (15:38)

In ancient times, a slave carried on his person the seal of his master. The fringes are the sign and seal of our servitude and submission to our Master, the Holy One, blessed be He.

Tosafot, Menaḥot 43b

"Look at it and recall all the commandments of the Lord and observe them." (15:39)

Seeing leads to remembering and remembering leads to action.

Talmud, Menaḥot 43b

"Look at it [*Oto*]." (15:39)

Oto ("it") also means Him. When the Israelites glance at the fringes they should feel as though the Divine Presence were resting upon them.

Tanḥuma Buber, Shelaḥ 37b

"Recall all the commandments." (15:39)

This may be illustrated by the parable about a man who was cast into the sea. The captain threw a rope to him and said, "Grasp this rope with your hand and don't let go for if you do, you will lose your life." Similarly, God said to Israel: "So long as you cling to the commandments you will survive."

Tanḥuma, Shelaḥ 15

"I, the Lord, am your God who brought you out of the land of Egypt to be your God: I, the Lord, am your God." (15:41)

Why is "I, the Lord, am your God" repeated? This is to teach us that God is our Sovereign at all times and under all circumstances. He has a claim on us which He will never relinquish. The people of Israel can never repudiate their relationship to Him who redeemed them from Egypt . . . "I, the Lord, am your God" at all times and under all circumstances.*

Sifre, Numbers 115

Reflection

Israel has a rendezvous with eternity. It cannot disappear for it is bound to God with an indissoluble covenant. We can defy that covenant and flaunt it but we cannot deny it. Many, like Ezekiel's contemporaries, would follow pagan ways and say, "We will be as the nations, as the families of the countries who serve wood and stone" (Ezekiel 20:32). They are reminded of their origin and destiny as Jews, as they realize that in all ages Jews are "brothers in distress." But it is not enough to feel that Judaism is a shared pain and peril. We are not only driven together by a feeling of

---

* For the significance of the Exodus in Jewish tradition and in the liturgy, see pp. 75-77, and Appendix, pp. 152-153.

common peril. We are also drawn together by a common purpose, by the pursuit of common ideals, and by a shared vision of a world at peace. We can confer a lasting benediction on the world by demonstrating our love of God through love for our fellow men.

The two blessings after the evening *Shema*

The first of the two blessings, prescribed in the Mishnah (Berakhot 1:4) to be recited after the evening *Shema,* is *Emet ve-Emunah* ("True and certain it is . . ."), an affirmation of the principles articulated and implied in the *Shema*.

The second blessing, *Hashkivenu* ("Cause us . . . to lie down in peace"), is a prayer for protection against the perils and fears of the unknown future.

Emet ve-Emunah אֱמֶת וֶאֱמוּנָה

"True and Certain"

This is the epilogue to the *Shema,* and it is regarded as an obligatory element of the *Shema*. Like the *Emet ve-Yatziv,* the epilogue of the morning *Shema, Emet ve-Emunah* is a reaffirmation of our covenantal relationship to God and of the redemption from Egyptian bondage which brought our forebears "into everlasting freedom" *(le-Ḥerut Olam).*

Louis Ginzberg held that a brief version of the epilogue was originally the congregational response by means of which untutored worshipers who could not read the text of the *Shema* affirmed the reader's recitation of it by voicing their acceptance "of the sovereignty of God and their gratitude for the Exodus from Egypt." Later the epilogue was expanded to include a description of the wonders associated with the Exodus: the slaying of the first-born, the cleaving of the Sea of Reeds, and the acknowledgment of God as the redeemer of His people.* In the epilogue, God is praised for manifesting His presence and redemptive power in history. Other religions concentrated on nature worship and had an

---

* Louis Ginzberg, *Commentary on the Palestinian Talmud,* I, pp. 213-15.

undeveloped sense of history. Israel made a great step forward in moving from nature worship to worship of nature's Creator. This led to the abolition of the rites of magic and of the sensual and erotic elements dominant in heathen religions. Judaism's celebration of God's role and rule in history transformed Passover, Shavuot, and Sukkot, which were originally nature festivals, into commemorations of peak events in the early history of Israel: the redemption from bondage (Passover), the Giving of the Torah (Shavuot), and the protection of Israel during the long trek through the Sinai wilderness (Sukkot).

The Greeks and many other ancient peoples conceived of history as being cyclical in nature, that is, consisting of an endless recurrence of processes and events. Millar Burrows compares the Biblical conception of history to a graph, with many ups and downs, but with a clearly perceptible trend and a progressive catastrophic conflagration despite the frequent prophetic warnings of an overwhelming doom. There is always the overarching concept of a new heaven and a new earth in which we will be ruled by righteousness. ''In human history the one eternal living God is working out His own sovereign purpose for the good of His creatures, first for His chosen people and through them for the rest of mankind . . . At the darkest hour, when human pride and self-will seem to have completely frustrated the divine program through the destruction of the chosen nation because of its refusal to follow the guidance given through lawgiver, prophet, and sage, the note of a promise, the assurance of another new beginning . . . sounds more strongly than ever.''*

Emet ve-Emunah closes with the words: ''Blessed art Thou, O Lord, who redeemed Israel'' *(Gaal Yisrael).* Hence, it is liturgically designated as *Geulah* (prayer of redemption).

We have said above that the third paragraph of the *Shema,* dealing with the law of the fringes, does not apply at night-time because the fringes were obligatory only during the day, when one could ''Look at them'' (Numbers 15:39). The early practice was not to read the third paragraph of the *Shema* in the evening. It was during that earlier stage that both the Mishnah (Berakhot 1:5) and

---

* Millar Burrows, ''Ancient Israel,'' *The Idea of History in the Ancient Near East,* ed. Robert C. Dentan (Yale University Press), p. 128.

the Tosefta (Berakhot 1:10) stipulated that when one reads the *Shema* in the evening one must "make mention of the Exodus." By this the Rabbis meant the *Emet ve-Emunah* which closes with the *Berakhah* of *Geulah*.*

Emet ve-Emunah in the evening *Shema* is the subject of the following Mishnaic comment by Rabbi Elazar ben Azariah, which is quoted in the Passover Haggadah:

> I am about seventy years and yet I never understood the reason for the reference to the Exodus in the evening service, until Ben Zoma derived it from the interpretation of the verse: "That you may remember the day of your departure from the land of Egypt all the days of your life" (Deuteronomy 16:3). The words, "*all* the days of your life," teach us that the Exodus must be mentioned also in the evening (Mishnah, Berakhot 1:5).

"Your children beheld Your Kingship."

The reference to the Exodus is climaxed by a retelling of the ecstatic experience at the Sea of Reeds when Moses and the people declared, "The Lord will reign for ever and ever" (Exodus 15:18). At the Sea, Moses and the people of Israel "beheld" the Kingship of God. Louis Ginzberg called attention to the special meaning that the Kingship of God *(Malkhut Shamayim)* has here as God's sovereignty manifesting itself in history. When tyrants are crushed, the faithful who are redeemed proclaim that God reigns: "The Lord shall reign for ever and ever."**

For our discussion on the Kingship of God, see pp. 84-86.

Hashkivenu הַשְׁכִּיבֵנוּ

"Cause us, O Lord our God, to lie down in peace"

Night has always been associated with gloom and fear. All the uncertainties and mishaps that fill the heart with apprehension

---

* In Palestine the *Geulah* began with *Emet ve-Yatziv* evenings as well as mornings. See Saul Lieberman, *Tosefta Ki-feshutah, Zeraim,* p. 12.

** Louis Ginzberg, *Commentary on the Palestinian Talmud, op. cit.,* p. 216.

loom extra large during the dark hours after man has returned from a day's toil. Pestilence stalks (Psalms 91:5), and those stricken with illness suffer piercing pains in the bones and ceaseless throbbing in the veins (Job 30:17). The king's couch needs to be encircled by sixty warriors all armed with swords because of terror by night (Song of Songs 3:8). Haunted by fear and plagued by guilt, man apprehends the voice of conscience more clearly during the night (Psalms 16:6). It is during the night that his actions pass in review before his mind's hall of memory. He is then more keenly aware of God's scrutiny of his conduct and is at ease only when he is sure that no unworthy motives have polluted his mind: "Thou hast tried my heart, Thou hast visited it in the night. Thou hast tested me and Thou findest not that I had a thought that should not pass my mouth" (Psalms 17:3).

Worry is the act of borrowing trouble from the future, and courage is the act of borrowing hope from the future.

Hashkivenu is a prayer for protection against the perils and fears of the unknown future. One of the by-products of religious faith is the hopeful outlook described by Isaiah: "The mind stayed on Thee, Thou keepest in perfect peace because it trusteth in Thee" (Isaiah 26:3).

"A canopy of peace."

On Sabbath Eve (and on Festival Eve) the closing blessing of *Hashkivenu* is, "Blessed art Thou, O Lord, who spreadest a canopy of peace over us, over all Thy people Israel, and over Jerusalem." This is a variation of the weekday blessing, "Blessed art Thou, O Lord, who guardest Thy people Israel forever." The reason given for this change is that on the Sabbath one enjoys extra measure of providential protection and one can therefore feel all the more confident under the Sabbath canopy of peace. However, an early Midrashic text indicates that in Palestine the closing blessing, "Who spreads a canopy of peace" was recited also on weekdays (Leviticus Rabbah 9:9). In Babylonia, *Hashkivenu* was concluded on weekdays as well as on Sabbaths with "Who guards His people Israel forever." In explanation of the use of the Palestinian "canopy of peace" version on the Sabbath, medieval commentators on the liturgy pointed to a Midrashic homily that the

Sabbath is itself a protection against peril and therefore would render the words "Who guards His people Israel forever" redundant (Midrash Tehillim 92:3).

Veshamru וְשָׁמְרוּ

"The people of Israel shall keep the Sabbath."
(Exodus 31:16-17)

Though this Biblical passage appears to be singularly appropriate here, questions were raised about the apparent disregard of the rule that the *Amidah* must follow the *Geulah* blessing without interruption (Palestinian Talmud, Berakhot 2d). It is for this reason that in the morning service *Ḥatzi Kaddish* is not recited before the *Amidah,* which follows directly after *Gaal Yisrael*. The Talmud even raises the question of why *Hashkivenu* follows *Gaal Yisrael* in the evening service, thus seeming to run counter to the rule. The explanation given is that *Hashkivenu* is to be regarded as a prolongation of the *Geulah* blessing (Talmud, Berakhot 4b).* Geonic scholars questioned the propriety of reciting the *Ḥatzi Kaddish* before the evening *Amidah*. Rabbi Amram was of the opinion that since the evening *Amidah* was held by some authorities to be optional, the rule of *Geulah-Tefillah* did not apply here (Tosafot, Berakhot 4b). The *Orḥot Ḥayyim* code unequivocally states this to be the reason. The Gaon of Vilna objected to the recitation of the Biblical verses inserted after *Hashkivenu* on Sabbaths and Festivals and on the High Holy Days, and his ruling is followed in most synagogues in the State of Israel.**

---

* Abudarham (Spain, 1340) says that *Veshamru* is recited after the "prolonged" *Geulah* to indicate that were Israel to observe one Sabbath properly they would forthwith be redeemed *(Nigalin),* as is stated several times in the Talmud and elsewhere (Shabbat 118b; Palestinian Talmud, Taanit 64a; Exodus Rabbah 25:12; Leviticus Rabbah 3:1).

** Leon J. Liebreich offered this alluring conjecture which discerns in the earliest structure of the evening service traces of the rule that *"Tefillah"* must follow *"Geulah"*: Inasmuch as the *"Tefillah"* was at first not obligatory, *Hashkivenu,* the second blessing following the evening *Shema,* was a personal *Tefillah* for protection from the dangers which lurk in the night.

Ḥatzi Kaddish ("Half Kaddish")

To mark the conclusion of the *Shema* portion of the evening service, the *Ḥatzi Kaddish* is recited here by the reader.

For a full discussion of the *Kaddish,* see pp. 68-71.

THE *AMIDAH*

The use of the word *Amidah* (standing) is post-Talmudic. In the Mishnah, the *Amidah* is designated as *Tefillah* (prayer), since it is the prayer par excellence, the recitation of which was deemed to be a religious obligation, though there was a difference of opinion about the obligatory nature of the evening *Tefillah*.

The Rabbis traced the origin of the thrice-daily recitation of the *Amidah* to the patriarchs. They said that Abraham originated the *Tefillah* of the *Shaḥarit;* Isaac the *Tefillah* of the *Minḥah;* and Jacob the *Tefillah* of the *Maariv*. The hours of the day when these prayers are offered were said by the Rabbis to conform with the hours when the regular daily sacrifices were offered in the Temple (Talmud, Berakhot 26b).

The Seven Blessings of the Sabbath *Amidah*

The *Amidah* of the weekdays originally consisted of eighteen blessings and is therefore designated in the Mishnah (Berakhot 4:3) as *Shemoneh Esreh* ("Eighteen"). On Sabbaths and holidays the *Amidah* consists of only seven blessings. The first three and the last three blessings of the Sabbath *Amidah* are the same as those of the weekday *Shemoneh Esreh*. In the Sabbath *Amidah* the thirteen intermediate blessings of the *Shemoneh Esreh* are replaced by a blessing called *Kedushat ha-Yom* ("Sanctification of the Day"). The omitted blessings are supplications for health, sustenance, and relief, concerns on which there is a cessation on the Sabbath since they are not in consonance with the calm and serenity of the day.

The order and content of the seven blessings are:

1. *Avot* ("Fathers")

We address God as "the God of our fathers, the God of Abraham, the God of Isaac, and the God of Jacob."

2. *Gevurot* (''Powers'')

We praise God whose omnipotence brings healing to the sick, relief to the distressed, who sends the rain to renew life in nature, and who decrees life and death.

3. *Kedushat ha-Shem* (''Sanctification of the Name'')

We acclaim the holiness of God whose name is hallowed daily by the celestial beings in the heavens above.

4. *Kedushat ha-Yom* (''Sanctification of the Day'')

God hallowed the Sabbath day as the crowning climax of creation. We pray that our observance of the Sabbath will be in accordance with His will and that we will serve Him with a pure heart.

5. *Avodah* (''Worship'')

We pray that the worship of our lips be favorably received, and that we may with our own eyes behold the return of the Divine Presence *(Shekhinah)* to Zion.

6. *Hodaah* (''Thanksgiving'')

We acknowledge and thank God for the extraordinary blessings of life and love which are the ''daily miracles'' bestowed on us by His beneficence.

7. *Berakhah* (''Benediction'')—*Shalom Rav*

We implore God, the sovereign Lord of all peace, to bestow peace on us and on all Israel, and to let His blessing of peace abide with us continually.

***Elohai Netzor* (''O God, guard my tongue from evil'')**

This prayer is not formally part of the *Amidah*. It originated as a ''personal petition'' by the fifth-century Babylonian sage, Mar bar Ravina. Several personal supplications were suggested in the Talmud as fitting conclusions to the individual's recitation of the *Amidah* (Berakhot 16b-17a).

COMMENTS ON THE TEXT

"O Lord, open Thou my lips." (Psalms 51:17)

This verse is recited to induce a devout mood and to attune the worshiper's mind and heart to the intent and content of the *Amidah*. In his commentary on the liturgy, Abudarham calls attention to the appropriateness of this verse since the two verses that follow it in Psalm 51 refer to the sacrificial worship which the *Tefillah (i.e., Amidah),* "the service of the heart," replaces. These verses are:

> Thou delightest not in sacrifices,
> else I would offer them . . . .
> The sacrifices of God are a broken spirit. (Psalms 51:18-19)

The *Amidah* must be recited in a proper frame of mind and not in a mood of sadness, indolence, levity, or hilarity (Tosefta, Berakhot 3:21). There are many Talmudic exhortations for proper devotion in saying the *Amidah*. Perhaps the most emphatic one is the ruling that one must stand before God with a feeling of awesome trepidation:

> Even if the king himself greets a man, [when he is saying the *Amidah* prayer] he may not return the greeting; and even if a snake were twisted around his heel he may not interrupt his prayer. (Mishnah, Berakhot 5:1)

In commenting on this, the Talmud relates this anecdote:

> Once, while a pious man was reciting his *Tefillah* by the roadside, an official of the Roman government passed by and greeted him. He did not respond. The official waited until the man concluded his prayers and then he said to him, "You worthless creature. Why did you not return my greeting when I greeted you? If I had cut off your head with this sword, who would have demanded your blood at my hands?" The man replied, "Let me appease your wrath with words. If you yourself had been standing before a mortal king and a friend had greeted you, would you have returned his greeting?" "They would have then severed my head with a sword," said the official. "If you act so," said the pious man, "when

standing before a human king, who is here today and tomorrow may be in the grave, how much more so I, who stand before the supreme King of kings, the Holy One, blessed be He, who lives unto all eternity!"

Talmud, Berakhot 32b

Barukh attah Adonai בָּרוּךְ אַתָּה ה'

"Blessed art Thou, O Lord"

The word *Barukh* is almost a refrain in the Prayer Book. The translation: "Blessed art Thou" employs the word "blessed" in the sense of "praised" or "praiseworthy." Jacob Emden (German Talmudist, 1697-1776), in the introduction to his commentary on the Prayer Book, equates the grammatical form of *Barukh* with that of *Raḥum* and says that as *Raḥum* means "the source of all love" (or mercy), so *Barukh* means "the source of all blessings." When we praise God, we do so because we are filled with an awareness of the transcendent Reality behind reality, and we pray to Him because we want to sense the nearness of God's presence. "The Lord is near to all who call upon Him" (Psalms 145:18).

Another nuance of the word *Barukh* is conveyed in the blessings of gratitude which are classified as *Birkhot ha-Nehenin,* in which we express gratitude for material, aesthetic, or spiritual delights. In such a context *Barukh* means "We thank Thee" or "Thanks are due to Thee."

Elohenu Velohei Avotenu אֱלֹהֵינוּ וֵאלֹהֵי אֲבוֹתֵינוּ

"Our God and God of our fathers"

Some think that religion calls for a renunciation of the mundane aspects of life or of involvement with society. With Whitehead, they avow that religion is "what a person does with his solitariness." But religion should not be used as an escape from the shared perplexities and concerns of the community. We must not permit an excessive mysticism to make us abdicate our moral and social responsibility. As Jews we address God as the "God of our fathers,'' who revealed Himself through the corporate self-awareness and collective experience of the people of Israel. Identifying ourselves with the spiritual quest that began with Abraham, Isaac, and Jacob, aids our personal quest for God.

The polarity of the individual's need for God, and of his duty to serve Him in the context of the historic experience of his people, is suggested in the verse, ''This is *my* God and I will glorify Him, *my father's* God and I will exalt Him'' (Exodus 15:2).

אֱלֹהֵי אַבְרָהָם אֱלֹהֵי יִצְחָק וֵאלֹהֵי יַעֲקֹב

Elohei Avraham, Elohei Yitzḥak, Velohei Yaakov

''God of Abraham, God of Isaac, and God of Jacob''

We address God not as our ''Ultimate Concern,'' nor as the ''Ground of Being,'' nor as the ''Spirit of the Universe.'' There are many ways and moods of conceptualizing God. But when we pray, we assert and reaffirm our determination to continue in our own life the tasks undertaken by Abraham, Isaac, and Jacob. ''Abraham, Isaac, and Jacob are not principles to be comprehended but lives to be continued,'' according to Abraham Joshua Heschel.

It is not a tribal exclusiveness that prompts our identification with the historic destiny of our people. When we recite a *Berakhah,* we address God as ''Our God, King of the universe.'' When we thank God for the food we eat, we thank Him ''who provides food for all living beings'' *(Noten Leḥem Lekhol Basar).*

A striking instance of the depth and breadth of the collective awareness that informs Judaism is the reply of Moses Maimonides to a question addressed to him by Rabbi Obadiah, a convert to Judaism. In his letter of inquiry, the proselyte said that he felt inferior to those born into Judaism. He asked Maimonides whether it was proper for him, whose ancestors were not Jews, to recite the blessings and prayers addressed to ''Our God and God of our fathers'' and those which speak of God, ''Who sanctified us with His commandments and chose us from among all peoples.'' Maimonides replied:

You should change none of these phrases but pray as any Jew prays whether you pray in private or whether you lead the congregation in prayer. Abraham our father taught the entire world and acquainted people with the truth and uniqueness of God. He brought many under the wings of the *Shekhinah* and taught them to keep the way of the Lord, as it is written in the Torah, "For I have singled him out, that he may instruct his children and his posterity to keep the way of the Lord by doing what is right and just" (Genesis 18:19). Therefore, every stranger who joins us, and everyone who recognizes the unity of God as taught in Scripture, is a disciple of Abraham our father; all are members of his household, for it was Abraham who brought them to the right path. . . There is no difference between you and us in anything . . . "Let not your descent be light in your eyes." If *our* descent is from Abraham, Isaac, and Jacob, *yours* is from God Himself; so it is expressly stated by the prophet, "One shall say: I am the Lord's; and the other shall call himself by the name of Jacob" (Isaiah 44:5).

Teshuvot ha-Rambam 293;
cf. Palestinian Talmud, Bikkurim 64a

הָאֵל הַגָּדוֹל הַגִּבּוֹר וְהַנּוֹרָא

Ha-Eyl ha-Gadol ha-Gibbor ve-ha-Nora

"The great, mighty, and awesome God"

The following anecdote reflects an earlier period when the text of the *Amidah* was still in a fluid state, and when the reader of the service was permitted to vary the text of each prayer providing that he concluded each element of the *Amidah* with the prescribed *Barukh Attah* blessing:

A certain person led the congregation in prayer in the presence of Rabbi Ḥanina. He prayed as follows: "O God! the great, the mighty, the awesome, the glorious, the powerful, the majestic, and exalted God." Said Rabbi Ḥanina, "Have you exhausted all the praise due to your Master? Were it not for Moses having used the first three of the attributes which you mentioned, the great, mighty and awesome God and for the Men of the Great Synagogue having fixed them in the liturgy, we should not venture to utter them. It is as if an earthly monarch had a million dinars of gold and one praised him for possessing much silver. Would this not be an insult?''

Talmud, Berakhot 33b

Rabbi Ḥanina was objecting to the proliferation and multiplication of adjectives in praise of God, because he regarded excessive laudation not as an act of piety but almost as one of blasphemy, in that such proliferation of words implied that it is possible for man to apprehend and express in words the infinite and incomprehensive nature of God. Hence he insisted that in the recitation of the *Amidah,* reference to God's majesty should be limited to the adjectives: *ha-Gadol, ha-Gibbor,* and *ha-Nora* (great, mighty, and awesome).

There are times when God seems to hide Himself and when a feeling of frustration and helplessness besets even the devout, as they fail to discern a meaningful pattern in the cataclysmic course of history. Such a feeling is described by Rabbi Joshua ben Levi with disarming honesty in this utterly frank passage:

> The Men of the Great Synagogue were so named, because they restored the Crown to its pristine glory. Moses said: ''The great, the mighty, and the awesome God'' (Deuteronomy 10:17). Then came Jeremiah and said, ''Alien peoples are occupying His Temple, where then are His awesome deeds?'' Therefore, in praising God he omitted the word *Nora* (awesome), saying only, ''The great, the mighty God'' (Jeremiah 32:18). Then came David and said, ''Strangers are oppressing His children, where then are His mighty deeds?'' Therefore when he prayed, he said, ''The great and the awesome God'' (Daniel 9:15), omitting the word *ha-Gibbor* (the mighty One). Then came the Men of the Great Synagogue and said: ''God is indeed mighty in that He restrains His wrath so as to give the wicked time to repent. He is indeed awesome in that, in the face of fierce persecution by

all the nations, His people has, through His power, survived." By what authority did Jeremiah and Daniel modify what Moses has enacted? Said Rabbi Elazar: "Knowing that God demands utter sincerity in prayer, they could not utter superlatives which did not echo their true feeling."

Talmud, Yoma 69b; cf. Palestinian Talmud, Berakhot 11c

When, in our prayers, we express faith in the power of God and in His goodness, we do not presume to see clearly the pattern and plan of His providential government of the world. Often, in moments of frustration and despair we are in the mood of exclaiming with the psalmist: "Nay, but for Thy sake are we killed all the day; we are accounted as sheep for the slaughter. Awake, why sleepest Thou, O Lord? Arouse Thyself, cast [us] not off forever" (Psalms 44:23-24). But then, we regain our composure and banish despair. Even though we do not yet understand the meaning of the agonizing events in which we are involved, we muster our endurance and call up our courage as, with the same psalmist, we say: "Arise for our help, and redeem us for Thy mercy's sake" (Psalms 44:27). Judaism enables such hope by its teaching that the individual Jew can play a meaningful, even if humble, part in the drama of history, by committing his life to the realization of the ideals which the prophets and sages of Judaism delineated as the grand obsession and divinely ordained purpose of the Jewish people.

Vezokher ḥasdei avot וְזוֹכֵר חַסְדֵי אָבוֹת

"Who remembers the pious deeds of the patriarchs"

The liturgy expresses concepts rooted in the Bible and the Talmud. When we say that God remembers the piety of the fathers (patriarchs), we refer to the Rabbinic concept of the "Merit of the Fathers" *(Zekhut Avot)*. This concept reflects a feeling of deep humility. To our forebears it appeared to be presumptuous and self-righteous to ask for divine mercy on the strength of one's personal merits. They felt less inhibited in prayer when they asked for merciful consideration on the basis of the "Merit of the Fathers." This "Merit" was an inherited spiritual treasury for them and for their "children's children," from which they drew courage in adversity and resilience in confrontation with persecution.

When in our prayers, we recall the piety of the fathers and the promises God made to them, we merge past and present in a continuum of vivid memory and indomitable hope. The life of an individual is transitory but God is eternal. Because the covenant with Abraham, Isaac, and Jacob is sealed with the seal of God's eternity, the individual's brief span of life takes on enduring significance when he links his life with that of the eternal covenant.

Umevi goel livnei v'nehem וּמֵבִיא גוֹאֵל לִבְנֵי בְנֵיהֶם

"And will bring a redeemer [*Goel*] to their children's children"

This expresses the confident hope that God would be mindful of His covenant with the patriarchs and will in the future send to their descendants the hoped for redeemer, who would put an end to the exile and establish a universal rule of equity and amity. The ideal Messianic redeemer would be a scion of the royal house of David. Through the ages his spiritual qualities were popularly conceived in the light of Isaiah's glowing description of the God-inspired king who was to save his beleaguered people from the Assyrians, who had in 722 B.C.E. conquered and destroyed the northern Kingdom of Israel and who now threatened the very existence of the southern Kingdom of Judah:

And there shall come forth a shoot out of the stock of Jesse,
And a twig shall grow forth out of his roots.
And the spirit of the Lord shall rest upon him,
The spirit of wisdom and understanding,
The spirit of counsel and might,
The spirit of knowledge and of the fear of the Lord [moral integrity].
And his delight shall be in the fear of the Lord;
And he shall not judge after the sight of his eyes,

Neither decide after the hearing of his ears;
But with righteousness shall he judge the poor,
And decide with equity for the meek of the land;
And he shall smite the land with the rod of his mouth,
And with the breath of his lips shall he slay the wicked.
And righteousness shall be the girdle of his loins,
And faithfulness the girdle of his reins.
And the wolf shall dwell with the lamb,
And the leopard shall lie down with the kid; . . .

They shall not hurt nor destroy
In all My holy mountain;
For the earth shall be full of the knowledge of the Lord
As the waters cover the sea.

Isaiah 11:1-6, 9

In that vision the "shoot out of the stock of Jesse" cleanses the land of its moral corruption, crushes the evildoers, and establishes the rule of absolute justice so that even nature's law of tooth and claw is replaced by perfect amity between the strong and the weak. But in that same vision the redeemer of the people from exile is God Himself:

And it shall come to pass in that day,
That the Lord will set His hand again the second time
To recover the remnant of His people
That shall remain from Assyria and from Egypt . . .
And will assemble the dispersed of Israel,
And gather together the scattered of Judah
From the four corners of the earth.

Isaiah 11:11-12

Throughout the Bible, the term *Goel* consistently refers to God alone. The psalmist refers to God as "My Rock and my Redeemer" (Psalms 19:15). Isaiah speaks of Him as, "Our Redeemer, whose name is Lord of hosts" (Isaiah 47:4), and in another passage he refers to Him as "the King of Israel, and his Redeemer, the Lord of hosts" (Isaiah 44:6). The liturgy too is suffused with the concept of God as the sole *Goel* of Israel. In the morning *Geulah* prayer we say, "Our Redeemer is the Lord of hosts, the Holy One of Israel is His name," and the blessing concludes with "Blessed art Thou, O Lord, who redeemed Israel" *(Gaal Yisrael)*. The only exception is this phrase of the *Amidah* which speaks of the *Goel* whom God will bring to redeem the descendants of the patriarchs. This clearly implies that a human redeemer will be the emissary and instrument of God's redemption of Israel. The liturgical phrase "and He will bring a redeemer" seems to have been inspired by a verse in Isaiah which, as translated in Targum Jonathan, and as rendered in almost all translations, reads as follows:

> And a redeemer will come to Zion, and unto them in Jacob that turn from transgression, saith the Lord. (Isaiah 59:20)

This meaning is also implied in the opening passage of *Uva le-Tziyyon Goel*. However, the context clearly points to the rendering of the verse as:

> He [God] shall come as Redeemer to Zion, and to those in Jacob who turn back from transgression.

This rendering has also been adopted in the new translation of Isaiah (Jewish Publication Society of America, 1973).

In Rabbinic literature, the designation *Goel* is also applied to various Biblical personalities whom God sent to bring redemption to His people. Among those designated as *Goel* are: Miriam, Aaron, and Moses (Exodus Rabbah 26:1), Samson (Sifre, Deuteronomy 357), and Elijah (Pesikta Rabbati 4:1). At no time did the human *Goel* eclipse the prominence and pre-eminence of God as the Redeemer. This is emphatically implied in the Sabbath morning prayer, "There is none comparable to Thee, O Lord our God, in the world, neither is there any besides Thee in the life of the world to come; there is none but Thee, O our Redeemer, for the days of the Messiah, neither is there any like unto Thee, O our Savior, for the resurrection of the dead."

In Jewish tradition the Messiah is a human being through whom God will in the unknown future redeem Israel from exile and establish peace among all peoples. In Judaism the future is normative, rather than the past. The Golden Age lies not in the past but in the future vision of a noble perfected humanity and a redeemed Israel, both encapsulated in the concept of the Messiah, who is yet to come. The power and potency of this concept was demonstrated in 1943 when the embattled martyrs in the bunkers of the blazing Warsaw Ghetto, believers and skeptics alike, jeered at their brutal totalitarian foes as they expressed their invincible hope in the coming of the Messianic era when the ideals they lived for and died for would be realized:

> I believe with perfect faith in the coming of the Messiah; and though he tarry, I will wait daily for his coming.

''Ideals,'' said Carl Schurz, ''are like stars. You will not succeed in touching them with your hands. But like the seafaring man on the desert of waters, you choose them as your guides and following them reach your destiny.'' Jewish mystical literature is replete with ecstatic and other-worldly conceptions of the coming of the Messiah, and in Jewish history there have been many tragic and frustrating times when Messianic hopes were shattered on the rocks of reality. Gershom Scholem, with his meticulous and monumental scholarship, has enriched Jewish learning by researches into the alluring Messianic visions that inspired many generations and brought frustration to other generations which were victimized by self-deluded false messiahs like Sabbatai Zevi.

However, in the mainstream of Jewish belief and thought, the ideal world of the Messianic era was given a more realistic formulation. Samuel, the third-century Babylonian scholar, offered this rather modest portrayal of the days of the Messiah, ''The only difference between this world and the days of the Messiah will be the delivery of Israel from the oppression of foreign governments,'' and he said this to counter more mystical conceptions of the Messianic future (Talmud, Berakhot 34b). Maimonides depicted the days of the Messiah in similarly realistic terms in order to highlight the possibility of human self-realization in a world governed by natural law and perfected by man's obedience to the moral law:

> Let it not enter your mind that in the days of the Messiah anything in the world's system will cease to exist, or any novelty will be introduced into the scheme of the universe; the world will go on as usual. The statement of Isaiah, ''The wolf shall dwell with the lamb, and the leopard shall lie down with

the kid'' [Isaiah 11:6], is a metaphorical expression signifying that Israel will dwell in safety among the wicked of the heathens who are likened to wolves and leopards . . . .

The Sages and Prophets did not long for the days of the Messiah for the purpose of wielding dominion over all the world, or of ruling over the heathens, or being exalted by the peoples, or of eating and drinking and rejoicing; their desire was to be free to devote themselves to the Torah and its wisdom, without anyone to oppress them and disturb them, in order that they might merit the life of the world to come.

In that era, there will not be famine or war, jealousy or strife. Prosperity will be widespread, all comforts found in abundance. The sole occupation throughout the world will be to know the Lord. Hence, Israelites will be very wise, learned in things that are now hidden, and will attain a knowledge of the Creator to the utmost capacity of the human being; as it is said, ''For the earth shall be full of the knowledge of the Lord as the waters cover the sea'' [Isaiah 11:9].

Mishneh Torah, Hilkhot Melakhim, 12:1-4

Lemaan shemo be-ahavah לְמַעַן שְׁמוֹ בְּאַהֲבָה

"For Thy name's sake"

Rabbi Simon ben Lakish said in the name of Rabbi Yannai: ''The Holy One, blessed be He, linked His name with Israel. This can be illustrated in the parable about a king who had a key to a small treasure chest. Lest the small key be lost, the king attached it to a chain, so that were the key lost, the chain would indicate where it was. Similarly, God linked His name with Israel so that they might survive.''

Palestinian Talmud, Taanit 65d

This parable illustrates how in Judaism God and people are irrevocably bound to one another. ''You have affirmed this day that the Lord is your God . . . that you will walk in His ways . . . and that you will obey Him. And the Lord has affirmed this day

. . . that you are His treasured people'' (Deuteronomy 26:17-18). The glory of God's name is enhanced when Israel enjoys security on its own soil. The luster of His name is diminished when Israel suffers in exile. The mutual interdependence of God and Israel is mentioned throughout Scripture. After Israel was defeated at Ai, Joshua prayed, ''When the Canaanites and all the natives of the land hear of this, they will surround us and wipe our name off the face of the earth. What wilt Thou then do for Thy great name?'' (Joshua 7:9). Jeremiah makes the same appeal: ''Though our iniquities testify against us, O Lord, act Thou for the sake of Thy name'' (Jeremiah 14:7). When Israel is in desperate straits, the psalmist pleads, ''Help us, O God of our deliverance, for the sake of the honor of Thy name and deliver us and forgive our sins for Thy name's sake'' (Psalms 79:9). Ezekiel goes so far as to assert that these exiles who desired to be ''like the nations and tribes of other lands that worship wood and stone,'' would be redeemed against their own will and beyond their merit: ''You will know that I am the Lord, when I have dealt with you not as your wicked ways and your vicious deeds deserve, but for the honor of My name'' (Ezekiel 20:44).

When we appeal to God to redeem Israel ''for the sake of His name,'' we internalize deep sentiments which defy logical analysis. These feelings are given luminous expression in several places in the liturgy. Most moving indeed is the *Taḥanun* supplication:

O Lord, spare us in Thy tender mercies . . .
Let not the nations say, ''Where is their God?''
For Thine own sake deal kindly with us and delay not.

בָּרוּךְ אַתָּה ה׳ מָגֵן אַבְרָהָם

Barukh attah Adonai magen Avraham

''Blessed art Thou, O Lord, Shield of Abraham''

''Shield of Abraham'' has its Biblical source in the verse, ''Fear not Abram, I am a shield to you'' (Genesis 15:1).

The *Amidah* opens with the mention of the three patriarchs but the first blessing concludes with a reference solely to Abraham. In explanation, the Talmud cites assurance given to Abraham, "And you shall be a blessing" (Genesis 12:2) and reads into it the implication of a promise to Abraham that he alone would be mentioned in the conclusion of the first blessing (Pesaḥim 117b).

אַתָּה גִּבּוֹר... סוֹמֵךְ נוֹפְלִים
Attah gibbor . . . somekh noflim

"Thou, O Lord, art mighty forever; Thou . . . causest the wind to blow and the rain to fall . . . sustainest the living . . . supportest the falling . . . healest the sick . . ."

Because of its opening words, this blessing is called *Gevurot* ("Powers," "Might"). We usually associate might with the ability to harm, but here it connotes the power to heal. When Moses pleads for God's forbearance with Israel, he says: "And now, I pray Thee, let the power [*Koaḥ*] of the Lord be great, according as Thou hast spoken, saying: 'The Lord is slow to anger and abounding in lovingkindness, forgiving iniquity and transgression . . .' " (Numbers 14:17-18).

This blessing speaks of the power and might of God as it is revealed when He sustains the living, supports the falling, heals the sick, and releases the captives. His power is manifested when He brings down the rain to make the earth fruitful, and it will also be revealed in the resurrection of the dead *(Teḥiyyat ha-Metim)*. Human beings imitate the Divine when they too use their power for "sustaining the living, supporting the falling, and healing the sick." They then serve as messengers *(Malakhim)* of God, whom the psalmist extols as "Ye mighty in strength, that fulfill His word" (Psalms 103:20).

Meḥayye ha-Metim מְחַיֵּה הַמֵּתִים

"Who revives the dead"

The Mishnah (Berakhot 5:2) ordains that during the rainy season there be inserted into the *Gevurot* blessing, which speaks of

Teḥiyyat ha-Metim ("the resurrection of the dead"),* the reference to God as: *Mashiv ha-Ruaḥ umorid ha-Gashem* ("He who causes the wind to blow and the rain to fall"). This insertion is called *Gevurot Geshamim* ("The wondrous power of God as manifested in the rainfall").

The new life which rain causes to sprout from the earth was to the Rabbinic mind an intimation of the resurrection of the dead. Rabbi Yoḥanan (Palestine, third century) speaks of the three keys which God never turns over to anybody: The key to rain, the key to childbirth, and the key to resurrection (Talmud, Taanit 2a). Here we see reflected an amazement at the miracle of life.

Belief in resurrection is a corollary of the doctrine that every person is "an entire world" (Mishnah, Sanhedrin 4:5) and that he is of high and incalculable worth.

All Rabbinic allusions to immortality imply the resurrection of the body. This served to counteract a denigration of the human body by sectarians who were influenced by the Greek concept of the soul *(psyche)*. The Rabbis, averse to a strict dichotomy of body and soul, insisted that the body and the soul of a man are together held to account and this is strikingly expressed in a charming parable:

> Antoninus said to Rabbi [Judah the Prince]: "Body and soul can escape from divine judgment. How? The body can say: 'It was the soul that sinned, for ever since I separated from it, I lie in the tomb silent as a stone.' The soul can say: 'It was the body that sinned, for ever since I separated from it I am soaring in the air like a bird.' " The sage replied: "Let me give you a parable. A human monarch had a splendid park in which there were fine new fruits, and he stationed in it two keepers, one lame and the other blind. Said the lame man to the blind one: 'I see fine early fruits in the park; let me climb up upon you and we will get them and eat them.' So the lame man rode on the back of the blind man and they got the fruits and ate them. Sometime later, the king came and said to them: 'Where are the fine early fruits?' The lame man said, 'Have I

* Louis Ginzberg claims that the reference to the resurrection was inserted into this second blessing to counteract the Sadducees who denied this doctrine. He said that this explains why this blessing is designated as *Gevurot* and also *Teḥiyyat ha-Metim*. See his *Commentary on the Palestinian Talmud,* Vol. 4, p. 167.

> then legs to walk with?' The blind man said, 'Have I then eyes to see?' What did the king do? He made the lame man mount on the shoulders of the blind man and punished them together. So God will bring the soul, infuse it into the body and judge them together."
>
> *Talmud, Sanhedrin 91b*

That the concept of *Teḥiyyat ha-Metim* is more evocative than descriptive can be seen from the paradoxical statement of Rabbi Jacob, "Better one hour of repentance and good deeds in this world than the whole life of the world to come and better is one hour of contentment in the world to come than the whole life of this world" (Mishnah, Avot 4:17).

Max Kadushin characterizes belief in the revival of the dead as "an indeterminate belief." This is confirmed by the poetic overtones of Rav's word picture of the hereafter:

> "In the world to come, there is neither drinking, neither procreation nor preoccupation with business, neither jealousy nor hatred or rivalry, but the righteous sit with their crowns on their heads and bask in the splendor of the Divine Presence. (Talmud, Berakhot 17a)

Attah kadosh אַתָּה קָדוֹשׁ

"Thou art holy and Thy name is holy"

In this third blessing of the *Amidah,* known as *Kedushat ha-Shem* ("Sanctification of the Name"), we praise God, our Creator, "who is holy and whose name is holy."

In contrast to the second blessing, which deals with physical phenomena (the wind blowing, the sick being healed, etc.), here we imply that God is *above* all such material conceptions.

Attah kiddashta אַתָּה קִדַּשְׁתָּ

"Thou hast sanctified the seventh day"

This is the prologue to the *Vayekhullu* verses which tell that God Himself ordained and sanctified the seventh day as a Sabbath of rest, recreation, and spiritual re-creation.

Vayekhullu וַיְכֻלּוּ

"And the heaven and the earth were finished" (Genesis 2:1-3)

As has already been noted, the recital of these Biblical verses is considered to be especially meritorious. They are interpolated into the body of the *Amidah* as the prologue to the *Kedushat ha-Yom*. Rabbi Ḥisda, a Babylonian sage (d. 309 C.E.), quoted Mar Ukba as having underscored the importance of *Vayekhullu:*

> He who prays *Tefillah* on Sabbath Eve and also recites *Vayekhullu,* is accompanied on his way home by two ministering angels. They place their hands on his head and say to him, "Your iniquity is taken away and your sin is expiated" (Isaiah 6:7). (Talmud, Shabbat 119b)

Abudarham and other medieval liturgists offer an attractive homily on the relevance of the verse from the Book of Isaiah cited by Mar Ukba. The Torah declares that it is a sin for one to refrain from testifying as a witness when he has knowledge of the circumstances surrounding a case (Leviticus 5:1). When one recites *Vayekhullu,* he testifies that behind creation is God the Creator. Had he failed to testify, he would have incurred guilt. Now that he has testified to that to which he is a witness, the sin which he might have incurred is taken away.

Jacob ben Asher (d. Toledo, *ca.* 1340) commends the practice of standing during the recital of *Vayekhullu* after the *Amidah* and during the *Kiddush*. He gives the reason that in Jewish law a witness is required to stand when he offers his testimony (Tur Oraḥ Ḥayyim 268). For the same reason, it is the practice in some homes that the person reciting the *Kiddush* stands during the *Vayekhullu* preceding the *Kiddush* and sits down as he resumes the *Kiddush*.

אֱלֹהֵינוּ וֵאלֹהֵי אֲבוֹתֵינוּ רְצֵה בִמְנוּחָתֵנוּ

Elohenu velohei avotenu, retzeh vimnuḥatenu

"Our God and God of our fathers, accept our rest"

On this, the *Kedushat ha-Yom* blessing, see pp. 129-130.

Kadshenu be-mitzvotekha קַדְּשֵׁנוּ בְּמִצְוֹתֶיךָ

"Sanctify us by Thy commandments"

The idea of the holy in Judaism

The word *Kadosh,* which is the key to this familiar and recurring phrase, means "to be set apart" and, hence, to be dedicated to God's service. We declare that our lives take on the dimension of holiness through the observance of the *Mitzvot.* God dedicated Israel to Himself by means of the *Mitzvot* and these transform it into a holy people.

One understands more clearly the implications of this concept if one attends to Max Kadushin's analysis of "The Commonplace and the Holy" *(The Rabbinic Mind,* pp. 167-188). He shows how the Talmud classifies certain objects as being intrinsically holy, these objects being for the most part associated with parchments containing the Name of God. They are actually called *Kedushah.* In the category of *Kedushah* are a scroll of the Torah, *Tefillin,* a *Mezuzah,* and scrolls of the Prophets or the Writings. In addition, the receptacles or covers for such holy objects, classified as *Tashmishe Kedushah* (accessories of holiness) must, like the *Kedushah* objects themselves, be treated with special reverence and not thrown aside carelessly (Megillah 26b). Apart from these objects of *Kedushah* and *Tashmishe Kedushah,* there is a second group of ritual objects which can freely be thrown away when they are no longer being used (Megillah 26b). They are known as *Tashmishe Mitzvah* (objects used in performing a *Mitzvah)* and are not intrinsically holy. A *Sukkah* is not holy after Sukkot, and the same is true of a *Lulav.* A *Shofar* or *Tzitzit* belong to the same category of *Tashmishe Mitzvah* in that, though they are used in the performance of a *Mitzvah,* they themselves are not considered holy.

This leads us to an important aspect of Judaism's concept of holiness. It is not the "ritual object" that is holy (unless it be related to that on which God's Name is written), but it is *man* who becomes holy when he performs a *Mitzvah.* This is clearly the meaning of *Kadshenu bemitzvotekha* ("Sanctify us by Thy commandments [*Mitzvot*]").

When we perform a *Mitzvah* we have experienced an event of

holiness and each *Mitzvah* is symbolic of the entire sacred system of *Mitzvot* whereby our lives partake of the dimension of the holy. For this reason the blessing before the performance of a rite begins with the mention of the sanctifying nature of all the *Mitzvot:* "Blessed art Thou, O Lord our God, King of the universe, who hast sanctified us by Thy *Mitzvot.*" Then the blessing continues with a reference to the particular commandment about to be performed.

The commandment is the medium for religious experience, a means through which we are imbued with a hallowed feeling. In Judaism, holiness is not a feeling of "otherness" or a "trip" or being "turned on." As we have seen, holiness is an experience induced by sacred acts *(Mitzvot)* which we dedicate to God, through which our lives are sanctified, and by means of which we become aware of His nearness. The Sabbath enables us to partake of a feeling of "normal mysticism," as Max Kadushin calls it, which comes from the celebration of the Sabbath as an event of cosmic significance and personal spiritual exaltation.

What is the nature and content of the *Mitzvot* whereby our lives are sanctified? What is the full meaning of the Rabbinic statement in which God says to Israel, "Be holy, for as long as you fulfill the *Mitzvot* you are sanctified, but if you neglect them you are profaned"? (Numbers Rabbah 17:7). It is commonly assumed that the *Mitzvot* are "ritual" observances, and this widespread impression seems to be confirmed by the fact that a *Berakhah* is recited only before the prescribed performance of some religious ritual, such as that of putting on *Tefillin,* entering a *Sukkah,* or sounding the *Shofar*. But these "ritual" *Mitzvot* do not at all exhaust the concept of *Mitzvah*. It is also a *Mitzvah* to give charity, to visit the sick, to show respect for the aged, to dower the bride, and to accompany the deceased to his final resting place. These righteous acts, no less than the ritual acts, make us holy. Why then do we not recite a *Berakhah* before such acts? A number of reasons have been suggested. One is that while ritual observances need a *Berakhah* to invest them with sacred significance, ethical acts are intrinsically sacred. Another reason is that one does not, as in the case of giving charity or visiting the sick, say a blessing for a *Mitzvah* occasioned by another person's misfortune. A third reason may be that the ethical *Mitzvot* devolve on non-Jews as well, and that a *Berakhah* is recited only on the performance of *Mitzvot* which are obligatory only upon Jews.

It is essential for a true understanding of Judaism that we avoid diluting the word *Mitzvah* by limiting it to the ritual observances, indispensable as these are. In the Bible it is made abundantly clear that righteousness must precede the observance of the rite. This idea is one of the main teachings of the prophets.

For additional discussion, see comment on Psalms 95:7, p. 35, and "Accepting the Yoke of the Mitzvot," pp. 86-88.

Veten ḥelkenu be-Toratekha וְתֵן חֶלְקֵנוּ בְּתוֹרָתֶךָ

"Grant our portion [ḥelkenu] in Thy Torah"

The word *Ḥelkenu* ("our portion") means "our lot." The Torah is the heritage of all Israel for it contains "the teaching with which Moses charged us as the inheritance of the congregation of Jacob" (Deuteronomy 33:4). It is therefore the supreme hope of everyone in the household of Israel to have his lot in life cast among those whose highest joy and preoccupation consists in acquiring an ever-increasing knowledge and ever-deepening understanding of the Torah. Maimonides rates the crown of Torah above that of priesthood and that of royalty, but what is distinctive about the aristocracy of learning is that it is available to every person, conferring upon him high worth regardless of how humble his birth may have been (Mishneh Torah, *Hilkhot Talmud Torah,* 3:1). Rabbi Meir said, "Occupy yourself less with business and more with Torah" (Mishnah, Avot 4:10), and the Talmud is studded with similar statements. Typical is this comment by Rabbi Yoḥanan at the completion of his study of the Book of Job:

> All living beings, man and beast alike, are destined to die. Happy is the person who was raised in the study of Torah and who labored in its study, for by doing this he brought pleasure to his Creator, earned a good name and departed this life with a good name. (Talmud, Berakhot 17a)

To warn their students against the intellectual arrogance which makes one disdain those who lack the capacity or opportunity to be distinguished in Torah study, the Sages of Yavneh would often recite this meditation:

> I am a creature of God and my neighbor too is a creature of God. My work is in the town and his is in the field. I rise early to my work and he rises early to his. As he cannot excel in my work, so I cannot excel in his work. Do not say, "I do much that is of high merit while he does less." We have been taught that it matters not whether a person does much or little, providing that he direct his heart toward Heaven. (Talmud, Berakhot 17a)

Rabban Gamliel even decried exclusive preoccupation with Torah study. He said:

> Splendid is the study of Torah when it is combined with a worldly occupation, for toil in both of them puts sin out of the mind; but the study of Torah which is not combined with work falls into neglect in the end and becomes the cause of sin. (Mishnah, Avot 2:2)

וְטַהֵר לִבֵּנוּ לְעָבְדְּךָ בֶּאֱמֶת

Vetaher libenu leovdekha be-emet

"Purify our hearts to serve Thee in truth"

A realistic awareness of self-serving motives and distractions which dilute and distort the sincerity of one's worship and the integrity of one's moral conduct prompted this plea for a pure heart. David prayed, "Create in me a pure heart, O God, and renew in me a steadfast spirit" (Psalms 51:12). A pure heart converts prayer from a religious exercise into an enriching personal experience. A pure heart cleanses our interior being.

וְהַנְחִילֵנוּ . . . שַׁבַּת קָדְשֶׁךָ

Vehanhilenu . . . shabbat kodshekha

"And let us inherit Thy holy Sabbath"

This prayer asks that the Sabbath become for us a prized

possession. The Hebrew word *(Naḥalah)* implies a personal possession with which we will not part. For example, Moses tells Israel, "But the Lord took you and brought you out of Egypt . . . to be His very own people" *(Am Naḥalato).** One rarely thinks of so intangible a value as the Sabbath as being a possession but this is of the very essence of the Jewish religious life. We should value as our dearest possessions the knowledge and the insights which result from our study of Torah. "Happy is the man," says the author of the Book of Proverbs, "who has found wisdom and the man who has acquired understanding; for wisdom is more profitable than silver, and the gain she brings is better than gold. She is more precious than red coral and all your jewels are no match for her" (Proverbs 3:13-15). The Rabbis tell us that God told Moses that He had a beautiful gift in His treasure room. Sabbath is its name and this treasure He decided to give to Israel (Talmud, Betzah 16a).

Because Sabbath was so precious a gift, Rabbi Zadok (first century) composed a prayer for Sabbath Eve from which many of the phrases of the Sanctification of the Day *(Kedushat ha-Yom)* have been taken:

> Out of the love, O Lord our God, with which Thou didst bear Thy people Israel, and out of the compassion, O our King, which Thou didst feel for the children of Thy covenant, Thou didst give us, O Lord our God, this great and holy seventh day in love. (Tosefta, Berakhot 3:7)

The *Seder Rabbi Amram* includes this ancient prayer in its text of the Sabbath *Amidah*.

וְיָנוּחוּ בָהּ יִשְׂרָאֵל מְקַדְּשֵׁי שְׁמֶךָ

Veyanuḥu vah yisrael mekadshei shemekha

"And may Israel, who hallows Thy name, rest thereon"

God's name is sanctified by martyrs who publicly demonstrate their fealty to Him (Pesikta, Beshallaḥ 87a; Palestinian

* Deuteronomy 4:20; cf. Deuteronomy 9:26, Jeremiah 10:17 and 51:19; I Kings 9:29; Joel 2:17 and 4:2; Micah 7:14; Psalms 28:9; 74:2, 78:71, and 94:5.

Talmud, Shevi-it 35a). But one also sanctifies God's name in life by participating in a public worship service, an experience which is also called *Kiddush ha-Shem* (see p. 78). When we recite the *Kedushah* we say, "We shall sanctify Thy name in the world just as it is hallowed in the celestial heights." God's name is also hallowed whenever a Jew acts in utter honesty and integrity. An example of an act of *Kiddush ha-Shem* is related of Rabbi Samuel ben Sistrai. He found a jewel that belonged to the queen. He then heard a royal proclamation that the finder would be richly rewarded if he returned the jewel within thirty days and that he would be beheaded should he delay its return. Samuel deliberately returned the jewel after thirty days. When asked by the queen the reason for the delay, he replied that he wanted her to know that he returned the jewel not "for fear of the queen," but for "fear of the King of the universe" who in the Torah decreed that found valuables must be returned. The queen then declared, "Blessed is the God of the Jews" (Palestinian Talmud, Bava Metzia 8c).

Another illustration of *Kiddush ha-Shem* is given about Simeon ben Shataḥ. He had bought a donkey from an Ishmaelite and found a jewel in the saddle. He immediately returned the jewel. The puzzled Ishmaelite said, "Blessed is the God of Simeon ben Shataḥ" (Deuteronomy Rabbah 3:3; cf. Palestinian Talmud, Bava Batra 13c).

Retzeh רְצֵה

"O Lord our God, look with favor on Thy people Israel and on their prayer"

This blessing is denoted as *Avodah* ("service") because it pleads for the restoration of the sacrificial order of worship in the Temple in Jerusalem. It is the oldest of the blessings of the *Amidah,* having originally been the prayer offered by the priests for the acceptance of their offering of the daily morning sacrifice (Mishnah, Tamid 5:1). With the destruction of the Temple, the text was altered by the addition of the phrase, "restore the worship to Thy Sanctuary," thus transforming the prayer into a supplication for the restoration of the Temple and its service. The concluding blessing originally read: "Blessed art Thou, O Lord, whom alone we worship in awe'' (Yalkut, Samuel 80). (It is still recited instead of, ''Who restores His presence to Zion'' in congregations where the Kohanim recite the priestly benediction.)

The communal sacrifices offered twice daily were regarded as concomitants of sincere repentance and as expressions of obedience to God's will. With the suspension of the Temple worship, the Rabbis looked upon the restoration of the sacrifices as the effect of Israel's repentance and reconciliation with God. The association of repentance with restoration of sacrifices is clearly seen in the fifth blessing of the weekday *Shemoneh Esreh:* ''Bring us back, O our Father, to Thy Torah and draw us near, O our King, to Thy service and restore us unto Thee in wholehearted repentance.'' With the cessation of the sacrificial cults, the greatest stress was put on the indispensability of repentance as a means of nearing the day when God, whose Presence *(Shekhinah)* had gone into exile with His people, would return to Zion and again be worshiped by His people as in ancient times. The opinion was even ventured that one whose spirit is broken through remorse and contrition is deemed as meritorious as if he had gone up to Jerusalem, rebuilt the Temple, erected its altar, and offered the prescribed sacrifices (Pesikta de Rav Kahana, ed. B. Mandelbaum, p. 353).

The idea of the restoration of sacrifices did not at all impede the prophet in his inspiring depiction of a future era when sacrifices would be accepted universally from proselytes who would be assigned highly important functions in the Temple service:

> Also the aliens that join themselves to the Lord, to minister unto Him and to love the name of the Lord, to be His servants, every one that keepeth . . . My covenant; even [also] them will I bring to My holy mountain and make them joyful in My house of prayer; their burnt-offerings and their sacrifices shall be acceptable upon Mine altar; for My house shall be called a house of prayer for all nations. (Isaiah 56:6-7)

When we recite the prayers for a rebuilt Temple in a fully restored Jerusalem, we identify ourselves with our ancestors, who envisioned *Eretz Yisrael* as the homeland of a sacred community and Jerusalem as a shrine from which enlightenment would go forth to all mankind. References to the sacrifices can serve for us as a symbol of our duty to dedicate to God all that we have and are.

Yaaleh Veyavo יַעֲלֶה וְיָבֹא

"May our remembrance and that of our ancestors and the remembrance of the Messiah the son of David Thy servant and Jerusalem Thy holy habitation . . . ascend before Thee . . . on this day"

On Rosh Ḥodesh and on the intermediate days of Pesaḥ and Sukkot, *Yaaleh Veyavo* is interpolated in the *Avodah* blessing of the *Amidah*. Past and present are here merged in a continuum of historic memory and future redemption. Implicit in this prayer is the belief that God remembers what man resolves to bring to remembrance before Him. Out of the persistent hopes which we express in prayer, God fashions the future. Our generation has been witness to this truth, for the "remembrances" which Jews invoked before God during the past nineteen centuries have come to fruition in the renewal of *Eretz Yisrael*.

Yaaleh Veyavo is also part of the *Amidah* (with the exception of *Musaf*) and the Grace After Meals on Rosh Hashanah, Yom Kippur, Pesaḥ, Shavuot, and Sukkot.

Modim מוֹדִים

"We gratefully acknowledge Thee"

The root of the word *Modim* is used in this prayer with two meanings: affirmation and gratitude. First we affirm that God is "Our God and the God of our fathers, the Rock of our lives and the Shield of our salvation." Then we declare that throughout the generations thrice daily—evening, morning and noon—we offer thanks *(Nodeh Lekha)* for His protecting care and for His miracles, which are daily with us.

Modim thus expresses gratitude for our daily blessings, for all the blessings of life. We see in them miraculous manifestations of God's beneficence. God owes us nothing but we owe Him everything. Every living moment is a free gift from Him. The material, intellectual, and aesthetic satisfactions which come to us, the presence of our loved ones, the companionship of our friends—all these are, to cite a phrase in the *Birkat ha-Gomel,*

"God's gracious goodness to the undeserving." When, in our prayers, we place before God our needs, we only express that which surges forth from our hearts, but we rely on Him to do what is in accordance with His will.

Our sages warned against the tendency to regard prayer as a *quid pro quo* and against sure expectations that God would acquiesce in our wishes. Such a mechanical view of prayer, they believed, was suitable for pagans, who denounce and renounce their gods when their wishes are not granted, but it is improper for Jews, who should willingly accept God's decrees. This thought was beautifully expressed by Rabbi Akiva when he said:

> "You shall not do so with Me" (Exodus 20:23). This verse means, "You shall not deal with Me as pagans deal with their gods. They honor their gods only when good comes to them, but as for you, when I bring good upon you, give thanks, and also when I bring suffering upon you, give thanks." Thus David said, "I will lift up the cup of salvation and call upon the name of the Lord" (Psalms 116:13); and he says too: "I found trouble and sorrow, but I called upon the name of the Lord" (Psalms 116:3-4). (Mekhilta, ed. Horowitz-Rabin, p. 239)

We put our trust in God even when He sees fit to delay or deny the fulfillment of our prayers. Rabbi Eliezer, when he traveled, would recite this prayer:

> May Thy will be done in heaven above, give peace of mind to those who fear Thee, and do what is pleasing in Thine eyes. Blessed art Thou, who hearest prayer. (Tosefta, Berakhot 3:7)

To discourage prayers that appear to command God to bend His will to man's desires, the Rabbis said that he who calculates on a ready answer to his prayers, invites and invokes a scrutiny of his own sins and of his unworthiness (Talmud, Berakhot 55a).

The following prayer by Baḥya Ibn Pakuda (Spain, eleventh century) is an example of a wholehearted surrender to God's purpose.

> You know what is for my good. When I recite my wants, it is

not to remind You of them, but only that I may understand better how great is my dependence upon You. If then, I ask for things that do not make for my well-being, it is because I am ignorant. Your choice is better than mine and I submit myself to Your decrees and Your supreme direction.

A deep sense of obligation to God for even the most elementary satisfactions of life is underscored in this statement:

> One must not taste anything without uttering a blessing to God, for Scripture says: "The earth is the Lord's and the fullness thereof" (Psalms 24:1). He who partakes of the bounties of this life without saying a prayer is considered as if he had made unlawful use of that which belongs to God. (Tosefta, Berakhot 4:1)

Shalom Rav שָׁלוֹם רָב

"Grant abundant peace to Thy people Israel"

Shalom is the last word of the *Amidah* and its liturgical significance is stressed in this comment by Rabbi Levi:

> Great is peace, for all the blessings and supplications we invoke before God conclude with *Shalom*. The [evening] *Shema* is concluded with "He who spreads a canopy of peace," the priestly benediction closes with *Shalom*, and the *Tefillah* concludes with *Oseh ha-Shalom* ["He who makes peace"]. (Leviticus Rabbah 9:9)

Elohai, netzor leshoni meira אֱלֹהַי. נְצוֹר לְשׁוֹנִי מֵרָע

"O my God, guard my tongue from evil"

Bible and Talmud abound with admonitions regarding speech, an endowment that marks man off from other living creatures. A most heinous sin is the abuse of speech for talebearing, slandering, and humiliating others. It is a sin even graver than the three cardinal sins: idolatry, adultery, and murder

(Midrash Tehillim 52:2). Of the conveyer of calumnies, God declares, "He and I cannot abide together in the world" (Talmud, Arakhin 15b). The motive of the slanderer is to deflect attention from his own blemishes; he maligns others and imputes to them his own defects (Talmud, Kiddushin 70b). His poisonous words are contagious. They might be spoken in Rome and destroy a life in Syria (Palestinian Talmud, Pe-ah 16a). Rabbi Simeon ben Yoḥai once remarked that had he been standing at the foot of Mount Sinai, he would have prayed that two mouths be created for man, one for studying the Torah and one for his physical needs. On second thought, he changed his mind reasoning that if the world's stability is now so much endangered by the evil effects of man's malicious use of his tongue, how much greater would be the peril were he endowed with two tongues (Palestinian Talmud, Berakhot 3b).

Because "Life and death are in the power of the tongue" (Proverbs 18:21), and because the gift of speech is so often abused, the fifth-century Babylonian sage, Mar bar Ravina, composed a personal supplication with which to conclude the silent *Amidah*. This is one of several such supplications given in the Talmud (Berakhot 16b-17a).

The opening phrase, "Guard my tongue from evil," is derived from the psalmist's prescription for leading the good life: "Who is the man who desireth life and loveth days that he may see good therein? Keep thy tongue from evil and thy lips from speaking guile" (Psalms 34:13-14). This verse is the subject of an anecdote about Rabbi Yannai (Palestine, third century). A peddler who used to make his rounds in the towns in the vicinity of Sepphoris, would cry out his wares in the market places, "Who wishes to buy the elixir of life?" Eager crowds would gather around him. When he came to the village where Rabbi Yannai lived, the venerable sage heard the peddler hawking his wares. He invited him to come up and sell the elixir of life to him. The peddler said, "You and people like you are not in need of what I have to sell." Rabbi Yannai pressed him and the peddler came up and pointed to the passage in the Book of Psalms, "Who is the man who desireth life and loveth days that he may see good therein?" and to the very next verse, "Keep [guard] thy tongue from evil and thy lips from speaking guile.'' Rabbi Yannai readily admitted that though he had frequently read that passage, he did not come to know its deeper meaning till that hawker came and made its meaning transparently clear to him (Leviticus Rabbah 16:2).

A similar homily is recorded in the name of Rabbi Alexandri (Palestine, fourth century), but this homily also includes a warning against quiescence and unconcern. He quoted the passage, ''Guard thy tongue from evil and thy lips from speaking guile.'' Then he continued with the observation, ''Lest a person say: 'I have guarded my tongue from evil and now I can indulge in sleep,' therefore the psalmist goes on to say: 'Depart from evil and do good;' the word, 'good,' refers to the Torah to which Scripture alludes in the verse, 'I give you good doctrine, forsake not My Torah' (Proverbs 4:2)'' (Talmud, Avodah Zarah 19b).

Velimkalelai nafshi tidom וְלִמְקַלְלַי נַפְשִׁי תִדּוֹם

''And to those who curse [insult] me let my soul be dumb''

''The beginning of strife is as when one let out water, therefore leave off contention before the quarrel breaks out'' (Proverbs 17:14). In his prayer, Mar bar Ravina asked for the inner strength to exercise patience and restraint even under extreme verbal provocation. In such explosive situations, silence is the most eloquent response for it is better to be offended than to become offensive. There are times when righteous indignation is highly commendable, when words and acts of rebuke aim to rectify an evil situation of enormous gravity. The Rabbis tell us that when Moses smashed the tablets on which were engraved the Ten Commandments, God commended him, ''You did well to smash them'' (Talmud, Shabbat 87a). But anger in situations that call for forbearance will not make a punitive and corrective impact.

Those who refuse to be embroiled in a battle of words are commended by the Rabbis in this passage:

> Those who are insulted but do not insult others [in retaliation], those who hear themselves reproached and do not reply, those who perform good deeds out of love of God, and those who accept their suffering with joy, of such people

Scripture says, "But they who love Him shall be as the sun when he goeth forth in his might" (Judges 5:31). (Talmud, Yoma 23a)

Petaḥ libi be-Toratekha פְּתַח לִבִּי בְּתוֹרָתֶךָ

"Open my heart in Thy Torah"

Professor Ginzberg once remarked that close to eighty percent of the books that comprise the classical literature of Judaism deal with questions of decision-making leading to action. The purpose of study is primarily to lead the individual to a higher level of conduct.

When Rabbi Tarphon, Rabbi Akiva, and Rabbi José the Galilean visited a home of a colleague in Lud, many other scholars were present. They discussed this question: Which is more important, study or action? Rabbi Tarphon maintained that action was more important. Rabbi Akiva contended that study was more important. They took a vote and the decision was that study is more important because it leads to action (Sifre, Deuteronomy 41; Talmud, Kiddushin 40b). Judaism has a word for knowledge which is virtually untranslatable. That word is "Torah." Torah is more than the objective, disinterested acquisition and cataloguing of factual information or even the scholarly exploration of the multi-roomed mansion of worldly wisdom. These were deemed worthwhile insofar as they cultivate man's moral sensitivity and help to make him more fully human. Speaking of what God expects of man, Jeremiah says, "Let not the wise man glory in his wisdom, neither let the mighty man glory in his might, let not the rich man glory in his riches, but let him that glorieth glory in this, that he understandeth and knoweth Me, that I am the Lord who exercises mercy, justice, and righteousness on the earth, for in these things I delight, saith the Lord" (Jeremiah 9:22-23). Judaism goes beyond the formulation of ethical postulates and ideal ends. It is a religion of behavior as well as belief. The study of Torah aims to develop man's ethical alertness, to teach him to master himself rather than to rule over others. The very next words of Mar bar Ravina's prayer spell out the meaning of the words, "Open my heart in Thy Torah," for they are immediately followed by, "And let my soul pursue Thy commandments." The juxtaposition of *Torah* and *Mitzvot* is almost a refrain in the liturgy of Judaism and it testifies to Judaism's insistence that one's conscience must be backed up by one's conduct.

Yih'yu leratzon imrei fi יִהְיוּ לְרָצוֹן אִמְרֵי־פִי

"May the words of my mouth and the meditation of my heart be acceptable unto Thee"

The closing verse of Psalm 19, can be more correctly rendered, "May the words of my heart and the utterance of my lips . . ."

This verse originally marked the conclusion of the recital of the weekday Eighteen Blessings *(Shemoneh Esreh).* The Rabbis indicate how appropriate this verse of Psalm 19 is at this point. In the enumeration of the Psalms, some sages contended that Psalms 1 and 2 are one psalm; others counted them as two psalms but considered Psalms 9 and 10 to be one psalm. In either case, the present Psalm 19 was actually Psalm 18. Thus, the eighteen blessings of the weekday *Shemoneh Esreh* end appropriately with the same verse that concludes the nineteenth psalm, which in reality is the eighteenth psalm (Talmud, Berakhot 9b).

Why the *Maariv Amidah* is not repeated

The repetition of the *Amidah* by the reader serves to enable those in the congregation who are not familiar with the prayers to fulfill their liturgical obligations by listening to the reader as he recites the prayers and by responding "Amen" after each blessing. Why, then, does the reader not repeat the *Amidah* of the *Maariv?* The reason is that the recitation of the evening *Tefillah (Amidah)* was deemed by some sages to be voluntary rather than obligatory (Talmud, Berakhot 27b).

Why *Vayekhullu* is repeated after the *Amidah*

In the Sabbath Eve *Amidah,* the text of *Vayekhullu* is introduced with the prologue *Attah Kiddashta.* This conforms to the importance of *Vayekhullu* to be recited on Sabbath Eve, attributed to Rabbi Hamnuna (p. 16). When a festival occurs on a Sabbath the festival *Amidah* is recited, which does not contain *Vayekhullu*. Hence, it was enacted that *Vayekhullu* should be recited after the *Amidah*. As a result, the practice developed for *Vayekhullu* to be recited aloud also after the Sabbath *Amidah* for the sake of those who do not know the text by heart (Tur Oraḥ Ḥayyim 268). Another reason is that it would otherwise seem strange for *Vayekhullu* to be recited only when a holiday falls on a Sabbath (Tosafot, Pesaḥim 106a). Originally the *Attah Kiddashta* prologue to the *Kedushat ha-Yom* did not include all the three verses of *Vayekhullu*. Thus in Maimonides' text of the Sabbath Eve *Amidah,* the prologue concludes with "And thus it is written in Thy Torah," and the Biblical citation following it is only the third verse: "And God blessed the seventh day and declared it holy, because on it God ceased from all the work of creation which He had done" (Genesis 2:3). For this reason it was enacted that all the verses should be recited after the silent *Amidah*.

Magen Avot מָגֵן אָבוֹת
"Shield of our Fathers"

As has been said above, the reader does not repeat the evening *Amidah*. *Magen Avot* is preceded by the blessing, "Blessed art Thou, O Lord our God and God of our fathers, God of Abraham, God of Isaac, and God of Jacob, the great, mighty, awesome, and Most High God, Master of heaven and earth" and it is followed by the full *Kedushat ha-Yom* blessing (pp. 125-131). The three parts constitute an abridged Sabbath Eve *Amidah*. This seems to contradict the rule that an evening *Amidah* is not repeated. In speaking of *Magen Avot,* the Talmud relates that on Sabbath Eve the reader would "go down" to the lectern desk to recite the *Amidah* because of "a danger" (Talmud, Shabbat 24b). Rashi explains the *Sakkanah* ("danger") as follows: In Talmudic days it was not the practice to hold evening services in the synagogue during weekdays because the synagogues were located on the outskirts of the towns. Public services were, however, held on

Sabbath Eve. Since some who lived at a distance from the synagogue came late, the service was prolonged for their sake by means of the addition of an abridged *Amidah*. This prolongation kept the congregation in the synagogue until all worshipers could leave together. The *Sakkanah,* Rashi explains, was that demons lurk in synagogues and attack unaccompanied worshipers.

However, the word *Sakkanah* occurs many times in the Talmud and always in the context of some hostile government having prohibited the practice of Judaism. *Magen Avot* seems to have gone through the following stages of development and usage:

(1) In the first stage it was a "wineless *Kiddush*" and also was deemed to be in lieu of the silent evening *Amidah,* which was not considered obligatory (Palestinian Talmud, Berakhot 11d).

(2) In the next stage when the silent *Amidah* and the *Kiddush* over wine were instituted in the synagogue its recitation may have fallen into disuse.

(3) In the third stage, during a period of religious persecution *(Sakkanah)* when Sabbath prayers were prohibited, *Magen Avot* served as an abridged "underground" *Amidah* prayer.

(4) When the persecution was lifted, the full *Amidah* was reinstated in the service but the *Magen Avot* was still retained as a historic reminder of those dismal days of persecution. The original nature of the *Sakkanah* had been forgotten and Rashi suggested the "demon" danger as a possible explanation.*

Magen Avot is not recited on the first evening of Passover when it falls on a Sabbath, because on the first night of Passover Israel is considered to have special divine protection, by virtue of the Passover night being a *Lel Shimmurim* ("night of vigil"), when God Himself shields His people from danger (Exodus 12:42).

* Saul Lieberman, *Tosefta Ki-feshutah, Zeraim,* p. 34.

COMMENTS ON THE TEXT

"Our God and God of our fathers" are the same opening words as in the full *Amidah*. "Master of heaven and earth" is a slight variation from the full *Amidah* where it reads "Master of everything." "Heaven and earth" is a Biblical idiom meaning all creation. Thus "And the heaven and the earth were finished" means "the whole world was finished."

The following seven phrases in *Magen Avot* correspond to the seven blessings in the Sabbath *Amidah:*

"Shield of the fathers" to *Magen Avraham;*

"Who revives the dead" to *Meḥayyeh ha-Metim;*

"The holy God" to *ha-El ha-Kadosh;*

"For He favored them to give them rest" to *Retze vi-Menuḥatenu;*

"Him we shall serve with fear and awe" to the ancient form of the *Avodah* blessing still recited by the *Kohanim* when they bless the people;

"And we shall give thanks to His name with a summary* of the blessings" to *Modim;*

"Who sanctifies the Sabbath" to *Mekaddesh ha-Shabbat.*

***Kaddish Shalem*, (the "Reader's Kaddish")**

To mark the formal end of the *Amidah, Kaddish Shalem* (the "complete *Kaddish*"), also known as *Kaddish Titkabbal,* is here recited by the Reader. For a full discussion of the *Kaddish,* see pp. 68-71.

---

* The Yemenite rite reads *Meon ha-Berakhot* (God is the "Source of Blessings") instead of *Me-en ha-Berakhot* ("a Summary of the Blessings").

The Kiddush קִדּוּשׁ

The prayer of the Sanctification of the Day over a cup of wine is an integral part of the Sabbath evening meal. The third-century Babylonian scholar Samuel formulated the rule that *Kiddush* must be recited at the table where and when the meal is eaten (Talmud, Pesaḥim 101a). As has been mentioned above, a *Kiddush* without wine was in an earlier stage recited in the synagogue. "It is customary there [in Babylonia] that where there is no wine, the reader goes to the lectern, and recites one blessing which contains a summary of the seven [blessings of the Sabbath *Amidah*] and concludes it with "Blessed be the Lord who sanctified Israel and the Sabbath" (Palestinian Talmud, Berakhot 11d). The summary referred to here is *Magen Avot*. After the *Magen Avot* became part of the prolonged evening service, the *Kiddush* over the wine was introduced into the synagogue service. The Talmud is hard put to reconcile this practice with Samuel's rule that the *Kiddush* must be recited where and when the meal was to be eaten. The explanation offered is that the recital of the *Kiddush* was intended for wayfarers who would eat at the synagogue as guests of the community (Talmud, Pesaḥim 101a). Because the reader needs to recite *Kiddush* at his own dinner table, he asks a child to drink the wine so that the blessing may not be a blessing in vain *(Berakhah Levatalah)*.*

COMMENTS ON THE TEXT

Vayekhullu is not included in the *Kiddush* that is recited in the synagogue since it has already been recited during the *Amidah* and immediately after it. But *Vayekhullu* is recited at home for the benefit of those who have not attended the synagogue service.

---

* Tur Oraḥ Ḥayyim 269. It is interesting to note that *Kiddush, Havdalah,* and the kindling of the Ḥanukkah lights must be repeated at home even by the person who led in these prayers before the congregation. The synagogue was not allowed to displace the home as the main center and source of Jewish religious practice.

"Who hast sanctified us by His commandments."

See comment on "Sanctify us by Thy commandments" (pp. 126-128).

"And hast given us Thy holy Sabbath as an inheritance."

See comment on, "And let us inherit Thy holy Sabbath" (pp. 129-130).

"That day being the first of the holy convocations."

This alludes to Leviticus 23:1-44, which describes all the fixed times and sacred occasions of the year. Among them the Sabbath is listed first.

"In remembrance of the departure from Egypt."

Allusion is made here to the text of the Ten Commandments in Deuteronomy 5:6-18, where the Sabbath rest is ordained for slaves as well with the admonition, "Remember that you were slaves in the land of Egypt and the Lord your God freed you from there with a mighty hand and an outstretched arm; therefore the Lord your God has commanded you to observe the Sabbath day" (Deuteronomy 5:15).

"For Thou hast chosen us and hallowed us above all nations . . . and hast given us Thy holy Sabbath as an inheritance."

Israel deems itself chosen among all peoples because it feels itself privileged to live in the constant companionship of God by means of the observance of the *Mitzvot*. In all prayers that refer to Israel as the Chosen People, the idea is linked to a particular *Mitzvah*. In the *Kiddush,* the Chosenness of Israel is attested to by the divine love which was bestowed on it through the gift of the holy Sabbath.

"Who hallowest the Sabbath."

This is based on the Biblical passages, "And God blessed the Sabbath day and declared it holy" (Genesis 2:3; Exodus 20:11).

Alenu עָלֵינוּ
"It is our duty to thank God"

This prayer, ascribed to Rav, the third-century Babylonian sage, was originally the introduction to the *Malkhuyot* verses of the Rosh Hashanah *Musaf Amidah*. It is read throughout the year at the conclusion of each of the three daily services because it expresses Israel's sense of privilege at having been the first people to purge itself of idolatry. It voices the hope for the time when all mankind will abandon its idolatries, and when the world will be perfected by the universal recognition of the Kingship of God.

The reason for the gratitude to God that "He has not made us like nations of the world," is explicitly stated in the full text, which includes the words (in italics) that were expunged by medieval censors:

> It is our duty to thank God . . . that He did not make us like other peoples on earth . . . *in that they bow down to vanity and emptiness and pray to a god that cannot help,* whereas we kneel and bow and prostrate ourselves before the Supreme King of kings, the Holy One, blessed is He.

Al ken nekaveh lekha עַל־כֵּן נְקַוֶּה לְךָ
"We therefore hope in Thee"

Having expressed gratitude for our having been taught to abjure idolatry and acknowledge God's sovereignty, the prayer continues with the petition that paganism shall vanish, idolatry be abandoned, and that "all may accept the yoke of Thy Kingship."

Man's bondage to evil will end when all idolatries vanish and all people order their lives in obedience to the will and the law of God.

In the Middle Ages, martyrs who died for the "Sanctification of the Name" uttered with their last breath the words of this prayer. Joseph ha-Cohen, a medieval chronicler, in his "Vale of Tears" relates the following:

> During the persecution of the Jews of Blois, France, in 1171, where many masters of the law died as martyrs at the stake, an eyewitness wrote to Rabbi Jacob of Orleans that the death of the saints was accompanied by a weird song resounding through the stillness of the night, causing the churchmen who heard it from afar to wonder at the melodious strains, the like of which they had never heard before. It was ascertained afterwards that the martyred saints chanted the *Alenu* as their dying song.

COMMENTS ON THE TEXT

"It is our duty to praise the Lord of all things."

Gershom Scholem draws attention to the inclusion in this prayer of Jewish mystical expressions which had been brought over to Babylonia from Palestine. Among these expressions are: "Creator of the Beginning." *(Yotzer Bereshit),* "Seat of His Glory" *(Moshav Yekaro),* and "His Majestic Presence" *(Shekhinat Uzzo).**

"While we kneel, and bow down, and prostrate ourselves [*u-Modim*]."

Saul Lieberman has demonstrated that here *u-Modim* does not mean "and [we] give thanks" but, "and [we] prostrate ourselves."**

---

* Gershom G. Scholem, *Jewish Gnosticism, Merkabah Mysticism and Talmudic Tradition,* (New York, 1960), pp. 27-8, 105.

** *Tosefta Ki-feshutah, Moed,* p. 696.

"That unto Thee [alone] every knee must bend."

This is based on the verse in Isaiah (45:23), "Unto Me [alone] every knee shall bow, every tongue shall swear."

"Let them all accept the yoke of Thy Kingdom [Kingship]."

For a detailed discussion on the acceptance of God's Kingship, see pp. 83-86.

"The Lord shall be One and His name One."

Eḥad ("One"), here as in the *Shema,* means "alone" or the only one, and this verse from Zechariah 14:9 should be more correctly rendered: "In that day the Lord shall be *alone* [*i.e.,* He alone shall be King] and His name be the only one [to be honored]."

"Mourner's Kaddish"

This *Kaddish* doxology which, as we have seen, is recited at the end of every congregational service, is also recited by mourners after *Alenu* and after the recitation of a psalm. It contains no reference to death, but is, nonetheless, relevant as a mourner's prayer. It affirms the enduring significance of human life when it is dedicated to the sanctification of the Name of God. For a full discussion of the *Kaddish,* see pp. 68-71.

***Adonai Ori* ("The Lord is my light")**—Psalm 27

This psalm is read during the month of Elul and through the High Holy Day period until the festival of Shemini Atzeret.

Yigdal יִגְדַּל

"Praised and adored be the living God"

Scholars assume that the author of this poem was Daniel ben Judah Dayyan (Rome, fourteenth century). *Yigdal* summarizes the Thirteen Articles of the Jewish Belief formulated by Maimonides in his commentary on the tenth chapter of Mishnah Sanhedrin. While his prose formulation of the creed of Judaism was never read in public, since it had never been officially adopted, its rendition as a hymn, originally recited only at the beginning of the service, has also been used as a closing hymn.

Adon Olam אֲדוֹן עוֹלָם

"Eternal Lord"

This noble hymn gives exquisite poetic expression to the human quest for the living God. Originally, *Adon Olam* was read only on Yom Kippur, but it appears in many manuscripts (and in all printed editions of the Prayer Book) as an opening prayer at the beginning of the morning service. Like *Yigdal,* it became a favorite closing hymn. In some synagogues *Adon Olam* is recited only at the conclusion of the morning service, but in other synagogues it is also recited at the end of the evening service. The authorship is unknown.

APPENDIX

A standardized liturgy, collective awareness, and the individual worshiper—some additional comments (See pp. 73-74)

Judaism may be defined as a "liturgical religion" in the sense that its fundamental beliefs and basic religious values are reflected in the corporate prayers of praise and petition that were canonized in the Prayer Book. Originally only the prescribed "concluding forms" of the blessings were required. If the content and tone of a particular blessing of the *Amidah* were adhered to, the individual was free to improvise his own prayers, providing that he concluded with the required *Barukh Attah* formula.

In addition, Talmudic law gave the individual the freedom to express his personal needs and petitions *after* the *Amidah,* even if those personal petitions were as long as "the confessional prayers of Yom Kippur" (Talmud, Berakhot 31a). The Talmud records the texts of some of the personal prayers recited by various sages; and one of them, *Elohai Netzor* ("O my God, guard my tongue from evil"), was later incorporated for recitation after the silent *Amidah* for every day of the year (Berakhot 16b-17a).

Up to the time of Rabbi Amram (*ca.* 850 C.E.), and even for some time after the appearance of Saadiah Gaon's (*ca.* 925 C.E.) and Maimonides' (1135-1204) liturgical texts, variations and improvisations were in vogue. The communities under the influence of the Palestinian academies tended to be more lenient and even to encourage variations in the wording of the texts of the *Amidah* prayers. Among the *Genizah* fragments discovered by Solomon Schechter there are Palestinian versions of the *Amidah* dating from the ninth century with significant deviations from the standardized text.

When the "canons" of the more than fifty rites of the liturgy were finally closed, and standardized liturgy became universal, it became the practice of poets in various communities to compose *Piyyutim* (liturgical poems) which were inserted into certain sections of the fixed liturgy. Their inclusion in the service was not mandatory; in our time they are recited mainly on the High Holy Days.

* * *

The collective consciousness with which Jewish worship is imbued did not diminish the Jew's self-awareness as a person; rather, it enriched and deepened it. It sharpened his sense of personal accountability and moral rectitude since the individual Jew was taught that, "All Israelites are responsible for one another" (Talmud, Sanhedrin 27b).

Max Kadushin has made the striking observation that in Rabbinic usage the word *Yisrael* has a dual meaning: It connotes the entire people and it also connotes the individual Jew. Moreover, the individual's personal conduct is said to be so decisive as to affect the destiny of the world: "He who performs a good deed may tip the balance with regard to himself and the whole world toward the side of merit; while he who commits a sin may incline the balance with regard to himself and the whole world toward the side of guilt" (Tosefta, Kiddushin 1:13).

The strong communal consciousness expressed in Jewish liturgy induced in the individual Jew a heightened sense of identity with the fate and future, the destiny and hopes of his people. As we have already indicated, it also deepened his self-awareness, sharpened his feeling of personal accountability, and enabled him to live with a sense of regal dignity. The collective spirit of the prayers led him to view his personal life in the perspective of his people's pilgrimage through the corridors of history and in the light of a vision of a great universal redemption in the future.

The community spirit which infuses Jewish worship accounts for the importance attributed to praying in consort with a *Minyan* (a congregational quorum of ten adults). "He who engages in the study of Torah and in the performance of good deeds and who recites his prayers with a congregation, is considered as if he had redeemed God and His children from the exile and from the oppression of the nations'' (Talmud, Berakhot 8a). The individual who cannot attend public worship is advised to recite the prescribed liturgy ''in an acceptable time''—which is defined as the hour when the prayers are being recited by the community *(ibid.)*.

Although the sense of divine vocation was central to traditional Jewish thought, the collective self-awareness and communal identification, which we have been discussing, was by no means ''isolationist'' in spirit. It was a lofty universalism that inspired the sages to say that the seventy sacrifices prescribed for the seven days of Sukkot [Numbers 29:12-34], were offered for the well-being of the seventy nations of the world [Tanḥuma Buber, 78b]. The idea that significant benefits and blessings accrued to *all* humanity because of Israel's worship of God, was emphatically expressed in the Midrashic comment [Numbers Rabbah 1:3] that if the nations of the world had been cognizant of the great benefits wrought for them by the Tent of Meeting, they would have surrounded it with garrisons and forts to protect it!

The Exodus in Jewish liturgy—some additional comments
(See pp. 75-77)

True to its Biblical and Talmudic antecedents, Jewish liturgy contains frequent references to the Exodus:

1. The *Kiddush* prayers, recited on Sabbaths, Festivals, and Rosh Hashanah, characterize each of these occasions as, "A remembrance of the going forth from Egypt."

2. Among the Biblical selections inscribed on the parchments of *Tefillin* is the thirteenth chapter of the Book of Exodus, in which *Tefillin* are ordained, "As a sign upon your hand and a symbol on your forehead, that with a mighty hand the Lord freed us from Egypt" (13:16).

3. The morning *Shema* is followed by *Emet ve-Yatziv* and that of the evening with *Emet ve-Emunah*. Each gives details of God's direct redemptive role in the Exodus and leads to the climactic declaration of the Israelites at the Sea of Reeds, "The Lord will reign for ever and ever" (Exodus 15:18), as the prelude to the *Geulah* blessing.

4. In the morning service, the "Verses of Praise" *(Pesukei de-Zimrah)* include the recitation of the song which Moses and the people of Israel sang at the Sea (Exodus 15:1-18).

5. The Kingship of God, which Israel witnessed at the Sea, is reaffirmed in the twice-daily recitation of the *Shema*. The recitation of the first section of the *Shema* is interpreted by the Rabbis as reflecting our acceptance of the "yoke of the Kingship of God," and the second as reflecting our acceptance of the "yoke of the *Mitzvot*" (Mishnah, Berakhot 2:2). The third section concludes with the Exodus theme, "I, the Lord, am your God, who brought you out of the land of Egypt to be your God; I, the Lord, am your God" (Numbers 15:41).

6. On the *Seder* night the home becomes the scene of a festive rehearsal and joyful celebration of the Exodus, the main purpose being to acquaint the children with the story of the Exodus

and to make that event a perennial living experience. In the *Haggadah* the father tells his children, "We were slaves to Pharaoh in Egypt and the Lord our God freed us from there with a mighty hand and an outstretched arm." To underscore the abiding significance of the Exodus to each person, the *Haggadah* cites the Mishnaic rule that in every generation a person is obligated to regard himself as if he himself had been freed from Egypt (Mishnah, Pesaḥim 10:5). A high moment of the Seder is the recitation of the Mishnaic preface to the *Hallel*. In that preface, God is praised for having performed, "For us and for our forefathers all these miracles: He brought us forth from slavery to freedom, from grief to joy, from mourning to festivity, from darkness into a great light, and from bondage to redemption" *(ibid.)*.